D0906341

OVERTIME!

An Uninhibited Account of a Referee's Life in the NBA

---

by RICHIE POWERS
with MARK MULVOY

David McKay Company, Inc.

Library of Congress Cataloging in Publication Data

Powers, Richie.
    Overtime!: An uninhibited account of a referee's
life in the NBA.

    1. Powers, Richie. 2. Basketball officiating.
3. National Basketball Association. I. Mulvoy,
Mark. II. Title.
GV885.2.P676   796.32′3′0924   75–2356
ISBN 0–679–50545–8

For Ginger

FOREWORD

I must confess here and now that I am not the greatest basketball fan in the world. As a kid growing up in Boston, I watched the great Celtic teams—Cousy and Sharman, Russell, Havlicek and Heinsohn, the Jones Boys, Ramsey, Sanders, Loscutoff and Red the Cigar—all the time because I could sneak into the building by slipping a crumpled $1 bill to a certain ticket-taker with the initials T.T. As a young sports writer for the Boston *Globe,* I continued to watch the Celtics frequently because they were kind enough to mail me two complimentary tickets for each game.

However, I lost interest in the game when I moved to New York in 1965. I wasn't about to watch some guys called the Knicks, not after watching the Celtics all those championship seasons in Boston. In fact, I have seen only five live NBA games in the last nine years.

On the other hand, over that same period of time I have attended perhaps a thousand hockey games, heard another two thousand or so on the radio and watched another three hundred plus on television. And it was hockey that introduced me to Richie Powers in a very roundabout way.

Brad Hvolbeck is a real estate man in Greenwich, Connecticut, by day, and a hockey-rink rat by night. One morning last fall he called me to report that he had cracked a bone in his leg playing hockey against some overly aggressive high school freshmen. "Bobby Orr has bad knees, and Brad Hvolbeck has a busted leg," I said. "I'll bet that's the first time anyone ever mentioned Brad Hvolbeck and

Bobby Orr in the same breath." Brad laughed and then asked me if I'd have lunch someday with the husband of one of his associates at his real estate firm in Greenwich. "You probably know him," Brad said. "His name is Richie Powers, and he referees in the NBA." I didn't know Richie Powers personally, but I had yelled "Powers is a bum" on numerous occasions back in Boston. Brad explained that Richie hoped to write a book and wanted to bounce the idea off an outsider's head.

We met for lunch at the Westchester Country Club several weeks later. Brad was still on crutches, and Richie was on the run to another game in some far corner of the country. Richie said he wanted to do a book about Richie Powers the referee. "What do you think?" he asked. I told him that I honestly thought it would be a difficult thing for him to do as long as he was actively working as a referee.

"In a couple of years, when you've retired to the golf course, I think it could be a super book," I said. "Not now, though. You'll just alienate too many people."

But Richie was quite serious. "So what?" he said. "I'll just tell what happens, and if people don't like it, that's their problem."

I looked at him. "It's one thing to say that now," I said, "but you may feel differently when you read the drafts of what you said into the tape recorder."

Richie shook his head. "No way," he said flatly. "I've always been a stand-up guy. I don't back down. Listen, I don't peep through key holes. I won't write about booze and broads and all that stuff, because it's none of my business. What is my business, though, is what happens on the court. That—and only that—is what I want to write about. And what I will write about!"

Richie pulled a tape cassette from his coat pocket, handed it to me and asked me to listen to it. "Maybe this stuff's not interesting," he said. "Just tell me what you think."

I had to drive to a hockey game in Boston the next day,

so I listened to Richie's tape en route. And it was all there. Richie was candid, perceptive and relaxed. Better still, the material was extremely lively and detailed.

I called Richie from Boston and told him that I liked the tape. We met again when I returned home, and he gave me a tape of his most recent NBA trip: a three-game, three-night, three-city junket to Boston, Philadelphia and Toronto. To my surprise, the second tape was even livelier than the first. "I think you have something here," I told Richie. Then he suggested that we collaborate on his diary.

"Hold it," I said. "I'm a hockey writer—not a basketball writer."

"Good," he said. "You'll bring a detached view to the diary."

And so the book was born.

At the start I told Richie he had to maintain an honest diary. He had to take the tape recorder with him and talk into it every day. None of this sitting down at the end of a long trip and trying to remember what had happened six days ago. Also, I reminded him that everything was important, even the most picayune details. And, finally, I said there could be no retractions. If Richie said on Monday that Charlie Double-Dribble cost his team a game by taking too many stupid shots, he couldn't, on Thursday, say, "By the way, I talked to Charlie Double-Dribble before the game tonight. He's a pretty nice guy, so why don't we forget what I said about him the other night."

Richie agreed. "It will all be in there as it happens," he said.

And it was.

And now I want to thank a number of people who contributed to the project in various ways. Wally Exman, who is a lot slicker with an editorial blue pencil than a sand wedge. Peter Carry, the basketball writer at *Sports Illustrated,* gave me a crash course about life in the NBA. Pat O'Connor and Lillian Hunt deciphered the inserts, the deletions and the scribblings on the original manuscript and managed to type a legible copy. And my wife, Trish, kept Kelly, Kris and Mark Thomas out of my office while I worked. Special thanks also to Managing Editor Roy Terrell of *Sports Illustrated*, a tolerant boss.

Of course, Richie made it all possible. It's his book.

MARK MULVOY
Rye, New York
November 1, 1974

PROLOGUE

In the spring of 1973 I was afraid I had refereed my last game in the National Basketball Association. After fifteen excruciating seasons, after working about fourteen hundred NBA games and calling about thirty thousand personal fouls, after being called everything from a fat bush-league squirt to a deleted deleted-deleted, after traveling about two million miles in cars, trains, buses and planes, after blowing his trusty whistle some hundred and fifty thousand times on courts from Booth Bay Harbor, Maine, to San Diego, California, I thought Richie Powers was done.

I was only forty-two years old, and except for the spare tire around my waist that has earned me the distinctive nickname of Double D—that's Double Dewar's on the rocks, and skip the twist, please—I looked as though I was in pretty good shape. But in April I suffered a severe thigh injury while working a postseason playoff game. I first felt a slight twinge of pain in the top of my right thigh early in the first quarter of a Milwaukee–Golden State game at Oakland. I did not think the pain was anything to worry about, so I just wrapped the thigh with an elastic brace and continued my work. The next day I applied ice packs to the thigh, and the treatment must have worked because I felt no pain whatsoever the following night in Los Angeles when I took the court to officiate a game between the Lakers and the Chicago Bulls.

Refereeing is a game of stops and starts—indeed, the

longest distance a referee ever runs in one direction is probably sixty feet. Early in the first quarter of the Lakers-Bulls game I put a heavy strain on my right thigh while making a sudden stop. Pain shot through my leg. Terrible pain. More pain than I had felt since that day in the Bronx when a car ran over nine-year old Richie Powers and crushed his right foot. At the scorer's table Darell Garretson, the alternate referee for the game, noticed I was grimacing and began to take off his jacket, thinking I'd retire for the night. Foolishly, I didn't. I limped through the remainder of the first half, then wrapped a heavier brace on my thigh during the intermission and finished the game.

My next assignment in the playoffs was a game at Boston between the Celtics and the New York Knicks. I had kept ice packs strapped to the thigh for four complete days, and felt confident that my physical problems would not affect my officiating. The first quarter went perfectly. Then, in the middle of the second quarter, Jo Jo White of the Celtics was driving up court when Walt Frazier of the Knicks suddenly stole the ball. I was running alongside White, and when Frazier took the ball away I had to make a sharp U-turn in order to remain with the play. I planted my left foot and swung my right leg back and around. WHAM! I couldn't even lift my leg. Bob Rakel, the alternate referee, took my place on the court and I hobbled to the Celtics dressing room. Dr. Thomas Silva, the Celtics physician, examined the leg, looked up and said I was through. *Through!* A tough word to hear. Dr. Silva probably meant I was through for that game, but in my mind I thought maybe I was through for the remainder of the playoffs, all next season and, perhaps, forever.

As a kid, I always got A for courage and often Z for brains. As a referee, I have always been the same way. Instead of obeying Dr. Silva and forgetting about the game out on the court, I asked Frank Challant, the Celtics trainer, to tape me up and let me get back to work. Frank wrapped several ace bandages around my thigh and even wrapped a brace around my waist. I'm chubby anyway—some players call me the Fire Hydrant—but with all those bandages and braces around me I could hardly put on my pants. I stepped out into the hall and began to run up and down the corridor. The leg felt okay, so I went back onto the floor and replaced Rakel in the game.

It was a terrible mistake. I thought more about my leg than what was happening among the players. They were the No. 1 and the No. 2 teams in the East, and the winner of their series probably would—and, in fact, did—win the World Championship. And here was Richie Powers ready to be a hero at their expense. On one play I pointed the wrong way on an out-of-bounds call. I had said the right thing, but when I pointed the wrong way the players on both teams were thoroughly confused and temporarily lost their momentum.

At the half, Walter Kennedy, the commissioner of the NBA, came into the referees' dressing room. I tried to convince him that I'd be all right. He, in turn, tried to convince me that I'd harm the game and myself by trying to continue. He explained that the purpose of the alternate official was to prevent just this sort of situation. He was right, of course. I was tremendously depressed. What worried me most was that the injury had happened to the same leg that was crushed thirty-two years ago. My right leg already is a quarter of an inch shorter than my left; my right foot is two inches shorter than the left; and the circumference of my right thigh is more than two inches smaller than the left. I didn't know if the leg could take another serious injury.

Dr. Silva re-examined the leg and told me I had torn the quadraceps, which are the four muscles at the top of the thigh. He said he could actually feel the hole where the quadraceps had torn away. As he packed my right leg in ice from ankle to hip, I sipped on a can of beer that the Celtics clubhouse boy had generously provided, and listened to Johnny Most's broadcast of the game on the radio. I could tell that Richie Powers was not missed one damned bit on the court because of the job Sokol and Rakel were doing. Then I heard Most say that Havlicek had been hurt in a collision with Dave DeBusschere of the Knicks and was leaving for the Celtics dressing room. I jumped off the table to make room for Havlicek, but Dr. Silva pushed me back on. The doctor looked at Havlicek's right shoulder and asked John to lift his arm. Havlicek tried, but he couldn't lift it above his shoulder.

"Sorry, John," Dr. Silva said, "but I can't let you go back out there."

"The hell with that!" Havlicek said. "I'm going to play."

"John," I said, "I'll lend you one of my arms if you'll lend me one of your legs."

As it happened, Havlicek was relegated to playing left-handed the rest of the series and was very ineffective. I remember watching one play on television when Havlicek broke away from the field, took a clean pass from Dave Cowens and went up to lay the ball into the basket. However, he couldn't lift his right arm even to the level of his shoulder, and the ball rolled off his hands and trickled out of bounds. It was a tragic way for one of the game's great players to end his season. Without a healthy Havlicek, the Celtics lost the series to the Knicks four games to three.

I did not work again the rest of the playoffs. At home, in Greenwich, Connecticut, I tried to run every other day, but I had to stop after only two or three strides. Once the weather turned hot late in May I began to play eighteen holes of golf every day at the Westchester Country Club. I must have walked at least four miles a day, seven days a week. Every so often I tried to sprint down a fairway, but I immediately would feel that same pain in my thigh.

Then, toward the middle of August, my leg began to feel 100 percent better. Suddenly I was able to run fifty yards without feeling any pain at all. So three times a day—morning, noon and night—I ran twenty fifty-yard sprints, and not once did I feel any discomfort.

I called Johnny Nucatola, the NBA's supervisor of officials, and told him that I thought I might be able to work the 1973–74 schedule after all, but said that I would not make a final decision until after the referees' training camp at Carroll College in Waukesha, Wisconsin, in September. Then my wife, Ginger, and I flew to Naples, Florida, for a ten-day vacation. On my return, I went into New York to see Walter Kennedy about my contract. I was unhappy with the numbers that the NBA had offered me, but I told Kennedy that I would not be signing any contract until I was 100 percent convinced that my leg would stand up to the rigors of refereeing a complete schedule.

I also decided to start the taping sessions for this book at training camp. After all, that's where the season really starts for me. At the time, I remember hoping like hell that when the season finished I would be witnessing it from some place on the basketball court.

Tuesday, September 11

Johnny Nucatola welcomed seventeen veteran referees and about a dozen rookie hopefuls to the annual training camp for NBA officials here at Carroll College in Waukesha, Wisconsin. After lunch, the veteran officials held a private meeting at which they discussed the possibility of forming an association of referees, much like the NBA Players' Association. In my own inimitable style I told the others that the only group I belonged to was the Roman Catholic Church. I said I did not disagree with the intents of the group, but at the same time I respectfully declined their invitation to join. Then they asked me to leave the meeting, which I wanted to do anyway.

The veterans have hired Mike DiTomasso, a former referee who now is a lawyer, to represent them in their negotiations with Walter Kennedy. I also have hired DiTomasso to represent me, but he will handle my negotiations privately and not as part of any group.

Thinking about my future, I took the state of Connecticut's examination for a real estate broker's license last week. If I can't call fouls on NBA players this year, maybe I'll be able to sell them some houses with high ceilings. I'd rather toot my whistle, though.

Wednesday, September 12

It doesn't look good. I refereed a scrimmage among the Milwaukee Bucks, who also train here in Waukesha, and I stupidly tried to do too much too soon. Ten minutes into the workout my right leg began to throb painfully, and I got so mad at myself that I broke my whistle in my hands and walked off the court in disgust. Now I'm told that I also broke a chair and tried to kick down a door on my way to the dressing room. I hope some real estate firm back in Greenwich can use another agent.

Thursday, September 13

Bill Bates, the Bucks trainer, worked on my thigh and was amazed at the atrophy throughout my right leg. I explained about the crushed foot, but he was surprised that the leg had not regained more of its size, considering the fact that the original injury had occurred more than thirty years ago.

Bill asked me what sort of rehabilitation work I had done on the leg throughout the summer. I told him about golf, and that late in the summer I had run fifty-yard sprints every day. He shook his head. "What you've got to do now, Richie," he said, "is get a lead foot and swing the leg a couple of hundred times each day."

I discarded the idea because the boot weighs about twenty-five pounds and there's no way I'm going to lug twenty-five more pounds around this season. I'm going to keep the leg strapped and see what happens.

Friday, September 28

My leg survived the rest of training camp, and I went home and continued to exercise it by taking long walks.

And now, please God, let it stand up under its first official test—the Seattle-Portland exhibition game at the Forum here in Los Angeles. It's warm and humid outside, and the Forum is very warm inside. Better still, the Forum floor is extremely soft and well-cushioned. I couldn't ask for better conditions to test my leg; I'll work up a good sweat early and my leg will get very loose. On the other hand, I'm glad I'm not working in Cleveland or Chicago, where the buildings lack climate control and proper ventilation and, as a result, usually stay very cold all night. Crowd size is important, too. The bigger the crowd, the warmer the arena; the smaller the crowd, the colder the arena. As always, they expect a sellout crowd at the Forum.

Peter Carry, the basketball writer for *Sports Illustrated*, is following me around because of an article he is writing about basketball referees. The story is supposed to appear in a mid-October issue—I hope I haven't retired by then! NBA Films also has selected me to be the subject for a promotional film on refereeing that will be shown during halftime on one of the regularly scheduled CBS telecasts during the season. For tonight's game I'm fitted with a small microphone. As a preventive measure I'm going to wash my mouth out with soap before the game. I hope some of the players wash their mouths out, too. Otherwise, the transcription of some of our on-court conversations will make the White House tapes sound like Mother Goose rhymes.

The game went without incident. Not once did my leg feel as though it would buckle. In fact, it actually felt better after the game than it did before.

Saturday, September 29

The film crew met me at the airport in Los Angeles as I was leaving for tonight's exhibition in Oakland. In any other city a film crew of six people might have looked out of place taking movies of a short, stocky man walking toward a plane, but not in L.A. I told Peter Carry that I didn't like doing the film because it was time consuming and changed my normal routine on the day of a game. He knew I was putting him on. My ego is such that I was terribly flattered to be chosen as the lead in the film.

Once again I worked a game without any physical problems. Afterward, I returned to the Edgewater Hyatt House across the freeway from the arena and applied a plastic bag filled with ice to my thigh. A precautionary measure.

Sunday, September 30

My leg has survived three rigorous games in three nights, and my general mood has changed from depression to elation. For the third straight night I went forty-eight minutes without feeling the slightest twinge of pain. Late in the game Sidney Wicks of the Trail Blazers stole the ball off a dribble and darted down court. To stay with the play, I had to make an abrupt U-turn, almost similar to the turn I made in Boston when my right leg collapsed. This time I made the move without any problems—and let out a tremendous sigh of relief. I suspect I will celebrate a little tomorrow on the flight home.

Friday, October 5

I have spent most of the last five days on the course at Westchester, enjoying the Indian Summer weather. I played during midday, when the weather was warmest, with the temperature climbing to the low 70s. Westchester is a hilly layout, and I ran up a lot of those miniature mountains in an attempt to strengthen my leg. Right now it feels absolutely perfect. The only bad part about Indian Summer golf is all the leaves on the course; one day I lost two new

Top Flites in the middle of a leaf-strewn fairway. In the middle of the *fairway*. Cripes! My golf handicap, in one respect, is my golf game. I have a funny-looking swing that incorporates the worst features of the swings of some of golf's great players. For instance, I fly my elbow like Jack Nicklaus. I loop the club at the top of the backswing like Gay Brewer. I swing with the same flat trajectory as Lee Trevino. And I try to muscle the ball like Arnold Palmer, even though I don't have that many muscles. On the greens I have the yips, just like Sam Snead, on any putt longer than two inches. The guys I normally play with at Westchester wouldn't give me a tap-in putt even if it meant I'd win a two-year vacation in Samoa. Then again, maybe they would because then they wouldn't have to play with me for two years. My favorite hole at Westchester is the nineteenth, where John Glynn keeps my good ol' Double D.

One nice thing about refereeing is that it gives you a chance to travel places on someone else's money and see friends whose names are on your Christmas card list. Tonight's place is Fredonia, New York, and the friend is Lou DiMuro, the American League baseball umpire with whom I once worked in the International League in my baseball umpiring days. We cut up old times before the Cleveland-Buffalo exhibition game.

One night in 1961 Lou and I were working in Richmond, Virginia—Richmond was a dry town in those days—and after the game we went back to the drugstore in the Richmond Hotel, sat down at the counter and ordered a supply of 3.2 beer. When the drugstore closed about 1:00 A.M., I invited Lou to my room for a nightcap. No, not 3.2 beer. I got out my Dewars-filled flask and poured us a couple of doubles. Several doubles later the flask was empty. "I'll be right back," Lou said, running out the door and down the hall. Moments later he returned with a grin on his face. "Surprise!" he shouted. There, clenched in DiMuro's right hand, was a bottle of Dewar's. Perhaps that's when Double-D got his nickname.

I was a professional baseball umpire for five seasons. In 1958, after my first year in the NBA, I umpired in the Class D New York–Pennsylvania League for $150 a month and 3¢ per mile. The money didn't bother me. Compared to the other umpires I was rich because I also had an NBA job that paid me about $15,000 per year. Most of the other umpires in the league had to live on their meager baseball paychecks. In those days I was a better umpire than basketball referee, and by 1961 I had progressed from Class D to the Triple A International League, where the salary was a princely $400 a month and most of the traveling was by plane.

I had given myself a five-year plan in baseball. If I was not on the threshold of a major-league umpiring career at the end of the 1962 season, I would quit working two sports and concentrate solely on basketball. However, in the spring of 1962 I happened to meet two National League umpires, Al Barlick and Ed Vargo, one night in the coffee shop at the Statler-Hilton Hotel in Los Angeles. I was in L.A. for a playoff game, and they were in town to umpire a Dodgers series. We exchanged the usual small talk, and I told them I was going back to the International League to umpire again as soon as the basketball playoffs were over. Then I asked Vargo and Barlick if they had heard anything about Richie Powers the umpire—off-the-record, of course. They told me they had heard some talk that Richie Powers was too small to umpire in the major leagues. I wasn't surprised, but I was mad as hell. During that winter I had read a statement made by Cal Hubbard, the supervisor of umpires for the American League, in which Hubbard said he wanted all his umpires to be "ex-football players." Hubbard, of course, was an All-American running back in the stone age. Nevertheless, for the first time my physical size—or lack of it—was a real knock. My ability didn't matter anymore.

It took me a few months to check out the official reports on Richie Powers the umpire. When I found out that what

Barlick and Vargo had told me that night in L.A. was indeed the opinion of the people who hired major-league umpires, I promptly abandoned my umpiring career, midway through the 1962 International League season. As the last out was made in my last game, I punted my umpire's cap in the air. I didn't look back to see where it landed, and I have never looked back on that decision to quit.

The final exhibition game on my schedule was similar to the first three: painless and effortless. I'm ready. My October schedule calls for ten games. I feel well. I look forward to working a complete eighty-two-game schedule and hope to finish the season injury-free for the first time in five years. And if someone needs a house in Greenwich, my wife Ginger will be able to take care of him.

Tuesday, October 9 (Capital at Atlanta)

Opening Game. Day One. The Capital Bullets, formerly known as the Baltimore Bullets, and before that the Chicago Zephyrs, play the Atlanta Hawks, in earlier years the St. Louis Hawks, and earlier than that, the Milwaukee Hawks. Manny Sokol, my officiating partner, is one of the nicest—and also one of the kookiest—characters I've ever met. He's so kooky that the league ought to give him flight pay just for walking around. Manny runs around yelling, "I love it, I love it!" when people ask him how he likes being a referee. He also says, "Refereeing beats schlepping cases!" (Before becoming a referee, Manny hauled cases of Seven-Up out on Long Island.)

I'm usually quick with the whistle, and even quicker with my thumb, in the area of technical fouls, but I set a record tonight by calling my first technical of the season less than two minutes into the game. Manny had called a foul against Phil Chenier of the Bullets. Instead of rolling the ball to Manny, or at least bouncing it toward him, Chenier held it defiantly, glaring in Manny's direction. Then he flipped the ball out of bounds. *Tweet!* I hit him with a technical foul for unsportsmanlike conduct.

Moments later Kevin Porter, Chenier's partner in the backcourt, mumbled something to me half audibly. I informed him that I would not listen to him. Then Porter said, quite audibly: "Let's call them both ways!" In the referee's parlance, that's being called a homer. *Tweet!* I hit Porter with a technical. Midway through the fourth quarter, with Atlanta pulling away to an easy victory, Elvin Hayes picked up the cudgel. I promptly warned him that he had no business addressing remarks toward me and advised him to cease and desist immediately. He chose not to take my advice. *Tweet!*

Listen. I call technical fouls in an attempt to maintain control of the game, not to build up the league's treasury. The players earn these technicals by abrogating their rights. In this instance, after calling the technical foul on Hayes, I told him to calm down. He answered, "Ah, throw me out." What else could I do? It was hardly a nice way to start a season.

When Hayes left the game, Wes Unseld came over and complained that Elvin hadn't used any profanity. I nodded and told Unseld that Elvin certainly had not used profanity in our discussion. I also told him that a player does not need to use profanity in order to break the rules.

Hayes, it seems, has become deeply involved in religion. After the game I happened to meet him outside the arena. "Richie," he said, "I prayed for forgiveness for myself, but I can't ask for forgiveness for you." "Elvin," I said, "I can appreciate the first part. But part two is absolutely silly."

Wednesday, October 10 (Seattle at Phoenix)

On the flight from Atlanta to Phoenix I read Wilt Chamberlain's book, *Wilt*. Chamberlain has definitely left the Los Angeles Lakers, and will be coaching the San Diego

Conquistadores in the American Basketball Association. Although Wilt had been the captain of the Lakers and thus had the right to discuss matters with the officials, he rarely involved himself with us. And when he did, his objections usually made sense. One thing I have always liked about Chamberlain is that when he wanted to discuss a call with me, he would bend down and address me eyeball-to-eyeball. This made the conference easier. Wilt is at least 7 feet 2 inches tall, compared to my 5 feet 10 inches—when he is in an upright position my eyes normally reach a point slightly above his navel.

Before the game I was introduced to Jack MacLeod, the new coach of the Suns. Jack says he wants to be called John. Maybe I should tell him I want to be called Richard. No, then they'd be calling me King Richard or Richard the Lion-Hearted.

I had seen Bill Russell, the new coach of the Supersonics, at the exhibition game in Los Angeles, but his appearance on a bench other than Boston's didn't register with me that night because I was too wrapped up with my thigh injury. At the captains' meeting before the tap-off tonight, Spencer Haywood of the Supersonics said to Jerry Loeber and me: "Bill doesn't want us talking to referees." It was nothing personal, of course. What Russell meant was that he felt it was a waste of time for his players to bitch to referees during a game. In other words, Russell would do the bitching, the baiting and the name-calling. He wanted his players to play basketball. In the NBA, that's a revolutionary idea. Even though Seattle was swamped by Phoenix, Russell hardly said a word to us. It was a peaceful evening.

Friday, October 12 (Capital at Seattle)

Russell was more vocal in his first appearance before the home crowd in Seattle. Early in the first quarter I gave the ball to the Supersonics after a Capital player had batted it out of bounds. I heard Russell say: "Good call, Richie. You got *that* one right." Then I called an offensive foul on Spencer Haywood and Russell reacted by jumping up and down in front of the Seattle bench. To me, it was too strong a reaction to a fairly flagrant violation, so I called a technical foul on him. After the Bullets converted the free throw, I had to put the ball back into play from a point in-front-of the Sonics' bench, perhaps two feet from Russell's seat. I expected Russell to say something humorous, because Russell always seems to find humor at the end of a tense situation, so I looked at him. When I did, his eyes rolled up—and he stared at the roof. I laughed.

In the end, though, Russell had his first victory as Seattle's coach as the Bullets—with a chance to win the game themselves—had two good shots roll off the rim in the final seconds.

Saturday, October 13 (Milwaukee at Golden State)

Jerry Loeber and I flew from Seattle to San Francisco in the morning, rented a Hertz and drove to the Edgewater Hyatt House in Oakland. Outside the hotel, confined to a small pen under the portico, was a princely looking mule wearing a green-and-gold blanket. It was Charlie-O, the mascot of the Oakland Athletics and their irascible owner, Charles O. Finley. The A's are playing my New York Mets in the opening game of the World Series, and Loeber asked me if I wanted to go to the Coliseum and watch the game. No way. I went to bed, put an ice pack on my leg, and watched the Oakland victory on the tube.

For the Warriors, the game against the Milwaukee Bucks would be their first of the season after two rain-outs. Yes, two *rain-outs.* Golden State was scheduled to play games earlier this week at Cleveland and Detroit, but the basketball floors in both cities were covered with water when the teams reported for the games. Trouble with the ice-making plants in both buildings, or so I was told. As I understand it, the warm weather outside, combined with the humidity inside, produced too much condensation, and the floors looked like swimming pools. I'm glad that the respective local managements had the sense to call the games and not attempt to play them at the risk of a potential serious injury to some player. Or referee.

The basketball rain-outs remind me of the time when I was the sole umpire for a Camera Day game in 1958 in the New York–Pennsylvania League. The Elmira club had sold thousands of tickets for the game, but it rained all morning and was still raining at game time. Packy Rogers, the best tobacco-chewer I've ever seen in action, was the manager of the Elmira Pioneers, and Zoilo Versalles was their star player. Rogers and the general manager obviously did not want to call the game, and insisted that the field was playable. I told them it was playable for ducks but not baseball players. I warned Rogers and the general manager that if they forced me to go onto the field, as they could, I would take the lineups from the managers and immediately call the game. "I don't care who breaks a leg," I said, "but it won't be Richie Powers." They decided to call the game before I could.

In the dressing room before the start of the Golden State–Milwaukee game, I reminded Jerry that we were about to referee a revenge game. The Warriors had upset the Bucks in the NBA playoffs last spring. I, for one, expected trouble on the court. Sure enough, it happened—early.

Rick Barry of the Warriors and Bob Dandridge of the Bucks always play one another very tough. Neither gives an inch, and they knock one another around pretty good. On one play I was standing underneath the basket and called a foul on Barry for hacking Dandridge. As I called the foul, Dandridge turned and knocked Barry's arm away. They both made menacing gestures, and then Dandridge turned his back on Barry. Suddenly Barry reached over Dan-

(*17*)

dridge's right shoulder and punched him solidly on the back part of his jaw.

All this happened in front of the Golden State bench, so the first person on the court was Al Attles, the Warrior's coach. Ever try to stop a steamroller? If I coached a football team, I'd play Attles at halfback on offense and middle linebacker on defense. Attles grabbed Dandridge to try to prevent him from getting back at Barry, who was in turn being smothered in Nate Thurmond's strong embrace. Somehow I managed to get Attles' attention, and told him that Barry was ejected from the game.

"Why only Barry?" Attles said.

"Nobody throws that kind of a punch and stays in a game," I said.

Barry yelled that Dandridge had hit him with an elbow. I had both players in my eyes throughout the play, and there was no elbow thrown. If I had permitted Barry to remain in the game after throwing that punch, I could have lost control of the game. And if the two of them had fought, they both would have been ejected. Listen. Once fights get violent—that is, away from the usual clutching and grabbing—the situation can get very dangerous. If the players want to fight, they're welcome to it out in the parking lot. The crowd did not appreciate the fact that I kicked Barry out of the game, but I did my job. I'm not out on the court to win a popularity contest.

The game continued without further incident, and the Bucks won by 15 points. Let's see. The season is only three games old, and I already have ejected Elvin Hayes and Rick Barry, two of the NBA's biggest stars. Believe me, I'm not proud of that. I don't get my kicks from putting down superstars.

My leg survived Week One in great shape.

Tuesday, October 16 (Buffalo at New York)

Like most NBA officials, I like to work games in my local area. For me, that means Madison Square Garden in New York City. I was born in Manhattan, grew up in the Castle Hill section of the Bronx, attended St. Raymond's Grammar School in the Bronx, LaSalle Academy on Second Avenue and Second Street in the Bowery section of Manhattan, and then St. John's University out in Queens. Now I live in Greenwich, about an hour's drive from Times Square. I only officiate six or seven regular-season games at the Garden each year, and I love them for all the obvious reasons: (1) I can leave home at five o'clock and drive to the Garden; (2) I can meet Ginger and some friends after the game for a peaceful dinner and a few Double Ds; (3) I can drive home afterward and get a long night's sleep in a familiar bed. Tonight I'm working the New York–Buffalo game at the Garden—round one for the unofficial New York State championship.

The Knicks riddled the young Braves with their poised and precise defense and pulled away to a commanding lead midway through the second quarter. At halftime Jack Ramsay, the Buffalo coach, indicated that he wanted to talk to me. Fine. However, according to the rules, if one coach wishes to talk to a referee during an intermission, the other coach—in this case, Red Holzman of the Knicks—must be present. But Holzman had already gone into the locker room, so I told Ramsay we would have to have the discussion after the intermission.

Ramsey wouldn't be placated. "Why'd you let New York play defense the way they did and not let us play the same way?" he suddenly blurted out.

That was no question. It was an indictment. So I did the only thing I could do—I walked away. Frankly, I don't know what psychological advantage Ramsay was trying to gain with that remark. Perhaps it was just the frustration of seeing his team being outplayed by a better one. The

Knicks are the defending champions of the NBA. They've played together a long time, and they live on defense. Buffalo is a young team, and probably will be champions of the NBA someday. Listen. I'd *gladly* allow Buffalo to play the kind of defense New York plays. Right now they're just not able to.

Wednesday, October 17 (Golden State at Milwaukee)

I'm supposed to be off today, but Johnny Nucatola has rescheduled me to work the Bucks' home opener against Golden State. I suspect that the NBA wants a seasoned official at the game, just in case some more fireworks erupt. So instead of a long night's sleep after the game at Madison Square Garden, I was up at 5:30 to catch a 7:55 flight to Milwaukee.

The Milwaukee papers are predicting another confrontation between Rick Barry and Bob Dandridge, but I'll bet they hardly look at each other tonight. Tempers always seem under control in the second round, and the players also realize that the officials are going to immediately respond at the first sign of another flare-up. Well, the Bucks struggled to victory as the Warriors seemed to be playing with a square basketball. There were no incidents whatsoever. No harsh looks. Barry and Dandridge were cool and collected. Let's see what round three will bring.

Al Attles, the Golden State coach, was strangely quiet throughout the game. In Oakland, Attles paces up and down the court with the play, not baiting the referees but just coaching his players. About two years ago, I reached an understanding with Dick D'Oliva, the Warriors trainer, and now when Attles departs on a sideline journey D'Oliva reaches out and grabs him by the coattails. Which reminds me of Bones McKinney, the old NBA star who once coached at Wake Forest University. Bones was very active around the bench when he coached the Demon Deacons and used to draw several technicals in every game for his gyrations. One night Bones developed the perfect cure for his hyperactivity: he had someone tie him to a chair beside the Wake Forest bench. He couldn't move anything except his lips.

Tuesday, October 23 (Los Angeles at Houston)

I'm very wary about what might happen at the Hofheinz Pavilion here tonight. Unlike most courts in the NBA, the floor at the Pavilion is one of those composition surfaces—that is, an amalgam of rubber and plastic and other synthetics that has a distinct tackiness. When you put your foot down on a composition surface you stop! When you put your foot down on the standard hardwood floor, though, there is a bit of give—that is, your feet spin, skid or slide slightly, thus reducing the shock of the impact. In a game a referee must do a lot of spinning to change his position, and spinning is considerably easier on hardwood than on composition. I figure that if my leg is going to collapse again it probabaly will collapse on a composition surface, such as the one at the Pavilion. So Ol' Double D may run a little daintily tonight, almost as though he's walking on eggs.

The Lakers beat the Rockets by a big score. And my leg held up under the stress and strain. I chatted briefly with Calvin Murphy, a Connecticut neighbor, after the game. When I speak at functions back home, people always ask me more questions about Calvin Murphy than Richie Powers. Next to Nate Archibald of the Kansas City–Omaha Kings, Murphy is probably the quickest player in the NBA and his quickness poses problems for referees. For instance, Calvin likes to drive the middle, a strategy that wouldn't seem to make sense—Calvin is barely 5 feet 9 inches tall, while the shortest center in the NBA is at least 6 feet 8 inches. Often when Calvin drives, he gets bounced around like a Ping-

Pong ball. The question for the referee is this: who's bouncing whom? Often Calvin winds up on the floor after bumping against a bigger player, and then he looks to me to call a foul on the defensive player. But it doesn't work that way. If Calvin bounces off a bigger player, then it's an offensive foul on him—or perhaps no foul at all. If he gets thrown to the floor, though, then it's a foul on the defender. We all have to be extra careful when the Murphys and the Archibalds invade the land of the giants.

Saturday, October 27 (Buffalo at Cleveland)

I've got to remember to wave hello to my family back in Greenwich. The Buffalo-Cleveland game this afternoon introduces the NBA on CBS after years on ABC. Ten days ago the CBS crew—Pat Summerall, Hot-Rod Hundley and Elgin Baylor—did the Bucks-Warriors game as a dress rehearsal. CBS will use the same time-out situations that ABC employed, which makes our job easier. The standard rule for time outs in a game is that each team must take one TO per period, with the home club taking its TO with approximately 6:59 to play and the visiting club calling its TO with about 2:59 left. For television contests, there is a mandatory third TO that the referee calls with approximately 4:59 to play. Neither team is charged with that TO, however. The maximum number of time outs permitted during a game is seven per team. However, no more than four time outs can be called by one team in the final quarter and no more than three time outs can be called by one club during the last two minutes of regulation time. If a game goes into overtime, each team is allowed two more time outs, which they can call at their discretion.

The first person I saw at the hotel was Sid Borgia, who was sitting in the lobby and reading a newspaper. Sid was the No. 1 referee in the NBA for years and now works for the league as an observer, studying NBA referees and scouting for promising young officials. As a general rule, Sid is not supposed to see me or any other referee before a game; in fact, he is even supposed to stay at a different hotel. Our meeting was an accident, but Sid nevertheless was quite upset that I happened to see him. He's supposed to be the invisible man. For some reason, the NBA doesn't want him to communicate with us at any time, not even after the game. Personally, I think the league is wrong here. Sid ought to come into the room after a game and tell us what he thinks we did right or wrong on the court. I mean, that's why he's there, isn't it? He can only help us by passing on his comments, pro or con.

Every time I see Borgia we always end up rehashing an incident that happened in Boston years and years ago. I had called a goal-tending violation against Bill Russell of the Celtics, thus arousing the ire of Arnold Auerbach. In those days a coach such as Auerbach could legally summon an official to his bench for a discussion about an official's decision. It was like standing before the mast. Auerbach asked me how I could have called a goal-tending violation against Russell.

"Red," I said calmly, "the ball had reached the apex of its parabola toward the goal, therefore Russell committed goal-tending." Then I walked away.

The next day one of the Boston papers printed a picture of Auerbach holding my arm and looking at Borgia in bewilderment. Red had said, "What the hell did Powers say?" And Borgia, just as bewildered, had replied: "Who knows? I never know what the hell he's talking about either!" As it turned out, I even called a technical foul on Auerbach for grabbing my arm.

CBS allots two hours and thirty minutes for each telecast, but the game—won by Buffalo—was over in two hours and five minutes, leaving Summerall, Baylor and Hundley with twenty-five minutes for idle chatter. After showering and dressing, I walked back toward the court and there were Baylor and Hundley still talking in front of a camera. I suspect the Nielsen ratings were a little low for those twenty-five minutes.

Sunday, October 28 (Philadelphia at Capital)

The Bullets are waiting for their lavish new arena in Largo, Maryland, to be completed, so tonight's game with the 76ers will be played at Cole Fieldhouse on the University of Maryland's campus at College Park. Before the game I ran into Jack McMahon, an old college buddy from St. John's, who played and later coached in the NBA. Jack advised me that he had been officially designated as Philadelphia's assistant coach and asked if he could sit on the bench. "Sure," I said. Then he said that the official papers about his appointment had not been filed with the league office and that several teams already had refused him permission to sit on the bench. I said, "I'll check with the Bullets coach."

I looked over at the Capital bench but saw only the assistant coach. Then I spotted Gene Shue standing at the scorer's table. "Gene," I said, "Jack McMahon has been named assistant coach of Philadelphia. Do you mind if he sits on the bench?" Shue laughed. "Sure, Richie," he said. "It's fine with me." Then he turned and went over and sat down next to McMahon on the Philadelphia bench. Suddenly, it dawned on me that Shue, who had coached the Bullets for the seven previous years, was now coaching the 76ers. Shue and McMahon were laughing as I walked over. "Hey, what town are we in?" I asked.

The Bullets chased the 76ers out of Maryland, winning easily. Doug Collins, the NBA's No. 1 draft pick, came into the game for the 76ers late in the second quarter and quickly committed four personal fouls. I had seen Collins at Kutsher's during the summer, and he looked then as though he'd be a super NBA player. Now he's hurt, and he's simply not quick enough yet to snipe the ball from experienced NBA guards. In the second half, right in front of the Philadelphia bench, Collins reached out for the ball and smacked a Capital player across the arm as he was shooting.

I naturally called a two-shot foul on the rookie. Collins jumped up and down in disgust. "I never touched him," he said, starting to bounce around like a kangaroo in heat. I said: "Hold it, son," but before I could say anything else, Shue, who was standing nearby, said, "You fouled him, kid. Leave the referee alone." Well, that stopped Collins' antics —and helped me. Collins had to be frustrated. But knocking an official, particularly when the official has made the proper call, will not get him, or anyone, anyplace.

Tuesday, October 30 (Los Angeles at K.C.–Omaha)

Happy Halloween! On paper, the Kings seemed to stand little chance of beating the Bucks because Nate Archibald, the NBA's scoring champion last year, is still recovering from a severe achilles-tendon injury. To compensate for Archibald's absence, the Kings have introduced a stalling offense that consumes at least 22 of the 24 seconds on the shooting clock before the first shot is attempted. Consequently we had a game of cat-and-mouse. Milwaukee would run down court and either fire away or lob the ball into Jabbar for an easy hook layup. Then K.C.–Omaha would respond with a yawn-producing dribble-pass-dribble attack. For a time Coach Bob Cousy's plan worked for the Kings, and they trailed by only 2 points at the end of the first quarter and only 7 at the half. However, Bob Dandridge and Jon McGlocklin both got hot in the third quarter and the Bucks pulled away to an easy win.

McGlocklin complained to me afterward that he had never seen such a deliberate, ball-holding game in all of his eight NBA years. He even suggested that the Kings had played an illegal zone defense against the Bucks. The last wasn't true. In recent years some NBA teams have refined the six to eight-foot "legal" zone defense, a strategy in which one player is allowed to cover another as long as he remains within six-to-eight feet of any opponent. The Kings employed a perfectly legal defense against the Bucks. Listen, as the Bucks proved in this game, you can beat any zone—legal or illegal—by fast breaking and good shooting. And every team in the NBA can fast break and shoot the lights out. You may see lower scores because of slowdowns, but there's one helluva difference between slowdowns and zone defenses.

Talking about Jabbar again, I was working an exhibition game in Hawaii shortly after he changed his name from Lew Alcindor to Kareem Abdul-Jabbar. On one play he asked me a question, and I said: "Lew . . . I mean Jabbar . . . I mean Kareem, I mean . . . ahhh!" Then Jabbar leaned down and said, "That's okay, Richie, at least you're trying."

Friday, November 2 (Golden State at Boston)

I'm leaving this morning on my annual foliage trip. Greenwich to Boston to Philadelphia to Greenwich to Toronto to Greenwich, all in less than sixty hours. Great way to spend a fall weekend, and it suddenly made me think: how many times have I gotten dressed and un-dressed during the last fifteen years? On the average game day I get up in the morning and get dressed. Later I get undressed at the hotel, take a rest and get dressed again for the game. Once in the locker room I change from my street clothes into my referee's suit, then after the game I change back again. At the hotel—after a few Double Ds—I get undressed again for bed. That makes a total of four dress-ings and four undressings each game day. I wonder what the Guiness Book of Records has to say about that. I guess I've gotten dressed and undressed ten thousand times dur-ing my career.

Saturday, November 3 (Capital at Philadelphia)

Another national television game, with the Bullets routing the 76ers, who were lucky to score 76 points. In keeping with the tradition established last week in Cleveland, I again helped get the game over in less than two hours and ten minutes, thus leaving the CBS crew with some twenty minutes of exciting fill time. The stage manager asked me to help them out by doing an interview with Hot-Rod Hundley and Elgin Baylor. However, NBA rules prohibit such interviews.

As I was leaving the Spectrum, I signed six autographs —making a total of thirty-one for the year so far, and that's ten more than last season's entire output. I still remember signing my first autograph back in 1957 after a game at the old Madison Square Garden. I came out the side door and a man asked me for my autograph, so I dutifully scribbled my name on the proffered scrap of paper. While I was talking to some friends, the same man came back and asked me for another autograph. "Didn't I just sign one for you?" I asked. "Yeah," the man answered, "but I need ten of yours for a 'Bob Cousy.'" I wonder how many "Richie Powers" it would take in today's inflated market to get a "Kareem Abdul-Jabbar"?

Sunday, November 4 (Chicago *vs.* Buffalo at Toronto)

The magic word in the NBA is a twelve-letter noun with very specific Oedipal references. When a player bestows the magic word upon me, I do a Groucho Marx imitation: "Congratulations! You have just said the magic word. Pay fifty dollars and haul off court. Pronto!" In the middle of the second quarter Randy Smith of the Buffalo Braves called me the magic word, and I summarily ejected him from the game. Herb Golden of NBA films happened to be in Toronto for the game, and he told me they had attached a microphone to Jack Ramsay, the Buffalo coach, during the game and there on the tape, loud and clear, was a strongly worded message from Ramsay to Randy Smith to the effect that you can't say the magic word to referees and get away with it. I applaud Ramsay for his actions. It was the first time I had been called the magic word all year, but I know one thing: it will not be the last.

Thursday, November 8 (Boston at New York)

Of all the rivalries in the NBA right now, nothing quite matches a Boston–New York confrontation, particularly at Madison Square Garden, where the crowd remains in a frenzy from the opening tap until the final buzzer. For three quarters tonight, though, the Celtics kept the Garden crowd silent by ripping through the Knicks with amazing ease. Without the injured Willis Reed, still suffering from an ailing knee, to worry about in the middle, the Celtics—particularly Dave Cowens and John Havlicek—repeatedly burst down the lane for unchallenged baskets. However, late in the game New York managed to score five or six straight baskets and reduced Boston's lead to about 15 points, triggering the up-til-then acquiescent crowd into action.

When I called a foul on the Celtics and signaled to the scorer's table I heard Havlicek say, "Don't let this crowd bother you, Richie." I was furious. "John," I said, "I'll pretend I didn't hear that." Listen. No crowd has ever bothered me. The crowd doesn't react until *I* do something. Or, as I like to say, "It ain't nothin' until I call it." Tonight, though, the crowd couldn't help the Knicks rally from their early deficit, and Boston scored a commanding win.

Havlicek, the quiet type, and I have had very few discussions over the years. I remember one time, though, when

John asked me why I had called a technical on one of his teammates. "For his actions," I said bluntly. "If a player waves his arms around me like an octopus, I tell him to put his arm down—or else I'll move mine. And when I move mine, it's a signal for a technical." John understood. Unfortunately, most people don't understand how ignominious it is to stand on the court and stare into someone's navel while that person is flapping his arms above you. All of which makes me wonder what the top of my head looks like. Come to think of it, the next time I have a discussion with some seven-foot giant, I think I'll ask him. That should stop the arm waving anyway, at least for a moment.

Sunday, November 11 (K.C.–Omaha at Cleveland)

The Richie Powers Show was shown on CBS yesterday, and I don't think I'll have to worry about any Oscar or Emmy nominations this year. How I watched it is another story. I was down at Lawrenceville Prep in New Jersey, watching my stepson, Rupe Johnson, play split end for the Lawrenceville varsity. At halftime Ginger and I walked over to Upper House, one of the dormitories, to watch the NBA halftime show. Tell me the last time you remember someone watching a halftime show. Anyway, by the time we had returned to the field, Rupe had caught a pass from the quarterback and galloped about 75 yards to complete an 86-yard touchdown play, which I'm told is a school record. We never saw it, and I don't think Rupe will ever forgive us. When I walked onto the court for the Kings-Cavaliers game several K.C.–Omaha players serenaded me with a whistled rendition of "Jesus Christ, Superstar." I bowed politely in their direction. Ah, the price of fame—or is it infamy?

The Kings beat the Cavaliers, who seem to be struggling. Jim Brewer, Cleveland's top draft choice, is having problems putting the ball through the basket, but he rebounds well and plays an aggressive defense. There must be a lot of pressure on the kid to be an instant success.

Wednesday, November 14 (Portland at Detroit)

I said good-bye, or whatever one says at 5:15 in the morning, to the family and flew to Detroit for the start of my toughest stretch of the season: five games in five nights, from Greenwich to Detroit to Phoenix to Seattle to Oakland to Los Angeles and then back to Greenwich. If all goes well, if my thigh holds up and my whistle doesn't break, I will referee my 1,000th regular-season NBA game Sunday night in Los Angeles.

On the road my days are invariably the same. I'm not one of America's great tourists. I don't visit museums or libraries or parks or other civic landmarks. When you've been to Detroit or Chicago or Seattle or Los Angeles fifty times or so, you almost feel like a native son every time you make another visit. I like to eat in the hotels or motels where I stay, and I'm a nut on room service. Basically I prefer the staples, like steak and eggs, and I try to avoid snacks. Around noontime each day I take a short stroll around town, just to get my legs moving. After that I go back to the room for an afternoon composed of dozing, reading, television watching and telephoning.

Like all officials, I carry the official NBA rule book with me everywhere I go and always look it over for about half an hour before each game. Nothing serious, just a brush-up on the rules.

I don't really psych myself up for each game. But what I will do is refamiliarize myself with the players in the game I will be working. As far as I'm concerned, there is no such thing as a "big" game. All games are equally important in my mind. Tonight, for instance, Portland plays at Detroit, and despite what most people think, this game is just as important as any New York–Boston or Milwaukee–Los Angeles game. Sure, the Trail Blazers and the Pistons have not won any championships, but their games are no less competitive than a Celtics-Knicks skirmish. In fact, a Portland-Detroit game is tougher to officiate than a Boston–New York game because the Trail Blazers and the Pistons generally make more mistakes than the Celtics and the Knicks; thus we must call more fouls. I'm not knocking them; it's a matter of official record.

Listen! Don't believe any of those statements from coaches who claim that the officials "let up" in games that don't involve the contenders. The first time I "let up" in a game it will be the last, because I will call Walter Kennedy immediately and inform him of my retirement. There is no such thing as an "easy" game for a referee.

Here's how "easy" the Portland-Detroit game was tonight. Early in the first quarter Bob Lanier of the Pistons went up to block a shot, and while he was suspended in midair he was hit from behind by one of his teammates and lost his balance. In an attempt to regain his balance, Lanier grabbed the rim of the basket and hung on it for about two seconds. Well, the rules stipulate that a player cannot grab the rim intentionally, which was what Lanier definitely did. At the same time Lanier's *intent* was to protect himself; he certainly did not grab the rim *deliberately*. A not-so-simple matter of semantics, because sometimes deliberately does not mean intentionally. However, I had no choice. I had to give Lanier a technical according to the strict interpretation of the rules. Weird? Well, I'm going to get in touch with the NBA rules committee and suggest that they let the referees use their discretion in such instances in the future. If Lanier had not grabbed the rim, he might have fallen heavily to the floor and seriously injured himself. In that regard, the technical foul was a small price to pay.

One of the most predictable things about NBA games is the fact that the second quarter will be 100 percent more hectic than the first. Why? The substitutes take over for a time in the second quarter, and they see themselves as potential superstars. And who's to say they won't be? So they go out onto the court to prove something to their coach and to the fans in an attempt to secure their jobs on the team. Consequently the quality of play often resembles schoolyard basketball as players forget their teammates and go one-on-one in an attempt to gain some personal recognition.

Sure enough, in the second quarter tonight John Mengelt of the Pistons and Mo Layton of the Trail Blazers were paired off on the court. Mengelt had the ball and drove the baseline, faked Layton high into the air, and then dove into him while throwing the ball toward the basket. Mengelt, of course, was hoping for a 3-point play but what I gave him was an offensive foul for charging. He was incensed, of course, and he made all kinds of gestures and gave me a verbal blast on the way down the court. As play continued, Layton had the ball and drove around Mengelt, who responded by slashing his elbow through the air. Fortunately, for Layton, Mengelt's elbow missed his head by a fraction of an inch. Moments later, Mengelt pushed Layton during some activity away from the ball. Time for Mr. Powers to act. I called Mengelt over and said: "I saw the elbow, and I saw the push, and if I see them again, you'll suffer for it." That ended that.

Later in the same period Mengelt happened to be guarding Geoff Petrie, and on successive trips down the court Petrie broke away from Mengelt for easy back-door layups. After each Petrie basket I noticed that Mengelt said something to Paul Mihalak, my officiating partner. Back in the dressing room at halftime I said to Paul: "Hey, I bet that Mengelt said that Petrie pushed him off." Mihalak laughed and said: "You are one hundred percent correct." Now this brings up another problem of sorts. Sometimes a player will complain to a referee that he has missed something, say a push, and will be completely correct. We can't see everything on the court. But in this case we both knew Petrie never pushed Mengelt.

Back at the hotel after the game, which the Trail Blazers managed to eke out in the last seconds, I bumped into a couple of National Hockey League officials. I had to laugh when they told me that one NHL linesman had been ordered to cut his hair so that his ears showed—or else. That's ludicrous. You don't blow a whistle with your hair. I remember once when John Nucatola noticed that an NBA official was wearing black gym shoes with white laces rather than the standard black laces. To Nucatola, this was a sacrilege. "The laces don't make the calls, I make them," the referee told Nucatola, but John was not amused. "Get black ones!" he ordered.

Thursday, November 15 (Philadelphia at Phoenix)

So traveling is fun? I got up at 6:15 this morning in Detroit, where the weatherman was predicting snow, and went to the airport to catch my flight to Phoenix. After boarding us on time, we were told there was an electrical failure on the plane. So I sat patiently, strapped into my first-class seat, for ninety minutes of "ten-minute" delays. I get tense during delays. I want to be in the city where I'm working before noontime on the day of the game. I don't want to arrive late in the afternoon, run from the airport to the arena and then dash onto the court. My metabolism can't handle it. I need my afternoons in the hotel room to relax, with time to call back home to make certain all's well with the family. All that helps relieve the pressure and the tension.

I was getting nervous about making it to Phoenix in time for the game, so I reached into my bag, took out my handy air travel guide and began to check on other possible connections from Detroit. All NBA referees are under strict orders never to check through their official's bag, the bag with their uniform, on a flight. We hand carry it with us wherever we go. There were no alternate connections from Detroit to Phoenix, but just as I was ready to push the panic button the flight attendant closed the doors and we headed for Chicago.

More bad news. Chicago was socked in by fog, and we circled for almost two hours before they found a hole in the clouds and landed. Thank God for radar. Two hours later we departed for Phoenix, and arrived at 4:00 P.M.—some five hours late. My only consolation was that the temperature in Phoenix was 74 degrees—and the weatherman couldn't even spell s-n-o-w.

I dashed to the motel, and the first person I saw in the lobby was Gene Shue, the coach of the 76ers. Another no-no. According to NBA rules, officials and teams are supposed to stay in different hotels at all times. The NBA does not tolerate fraternization between referees and coaches or referees and players. This was an accident, though, because Shue, unbeknownst to me, had shifted the 76ers from their usual hotel to my motel at the last minute. And there was no way that I was going to move to another motel at this hour. Let the 76ers move.

The Suns beat the 76ers in a contest that featured almost total ineptness by both clubs. For instance, neither the Suns nor the 76ers managed to hit on even 40 percent of their shots, a terrible average. In one space of eight seconds in the third quarter each team had the ball three times! Incredible. All night long it seemed as though the ball was a mass of silly putty.

I hate to disparage players, but the Suns and the 76ers were awful tonight. You know, referees are called inept, poor, butchers, idiots and a hell of a lot of unprintable things when players, coaches and fans think they have missed just one call. Well, tell me, on some given night aren't athletes really the same way? While I don't believe that referees can be poor or inept on any night, that they always should do their job to the ultimate, it is only natural that we have some nights that are better than others. Our problems, though, become compounded by the poor performances of the players, and then people have the nerve to say we've had a bad game. In this game all twenty-four players happened to have a bad night at the same time. Believe me, it's strange, to see these great athletes endure fleeting periods of frustration.

At least Doug Collins of the 76ers provided a few moments of comic relief late in the game. Collins had just scored a basket, and as he back-pedaled down court on defense, he suddenly vaulted high into the air in an attempt to convince me he had been charged by one of the Phoenix players. Actually, Collins was attempting to fool me. I admit that I can be fooled, but how often can it be done? I don't believe any player in the league can fool me more than once in his career. Anyway, Collins looked like Superman as he flailed away in midair. My first reaction was that someone had nudged him in the rear with a hot poker. I couldn't help smiling, and as I moved back up the court, I noticed that everyone at the scorer's table and along the press row was laughing like mad. Would you believe that on the very next play Collins repeated the same maneuver? Only this time he outdid his previous effort, setting what must be a new NBA record for the high jump. I thought he was auditioning for the Flying Wallendas. The only people who weren't laughing by this time were Collins and Gene Shue.

I saw Gene standing in front of his bench, shaking his head disgustedly. I went over and said, "Gene, I think your Mr. Collins is trying to outdo Sarah Bernhardt." I'm sure that Shue will take young Collins aside sometime and explain the facts of life in the NBA. I hope he does, anyway.

You know, games like tonight's inept contest bother me because they provide fuel for the critics who contend that expansion has diluted the talent in the NBA. Maybe it has, but at the same time expansion has provided more playing opportunities, and as a result has helped players fulfill their development, players such as Clem Haskins of Phoenix and Paul Silas of Boston, for example. Silas was a better-than-average player with the Hawks and the Suns, but he is a superstar now with the Celtics because at last he is playing for a team that needs him primarily for the things he does best—rebound and play defense. In Boston, Silas does not have to take twenty-foot jumpers and make them in order for the Celtics to win. If Silas rebounds and does his job defensively, he knows the Celtics will win. His offensive contributions are a bonus to the Celtics. However, with the Suns and the Hawks, Silas had to defense the opposition's toughest forward, control the rebounding, and *also* make all those twenty-foot jumpers for his team to win.

Friday, November 16 (Cleveland at Seattle)

More travel problems—in fact, getting from Detroit to Phoenix yesterday was simple compared to today's episode of traveling from Phoenix to Seattle. After less than four hours of bad sleep, I got up at 6:00 A.M., taxied to the airport, and checked in for the 8:15 American Airlines flight to Los Angeles that would enable Jim Capers, my officiating partner, and me to connect to our flight to Seattle.

The man at the check-in counter said, "Good Morning, gentlemen," took our tickets, stamped them and said matter-of-factly, "There will be a thirty-minute delay in departure because of a mechanical problem with the Number Two engine." We boarded the plane anyway, but they soon told us that the delay would last longer than thirty minutes. Good-bye to our connection in Los Angeles. Once again I whipped out my trusty airline guide and checked the alternate connection to Seattle. Continental Airlines had a flight out of Phoenix to Los Angeles with a connection to Seattle. Perfect. Jim and I grabbed our gear and ran to the

Continental terminal. "Sorry, sirs," a cute young thing said, "the nine o'clock flight to Los Angeles has been permanently canceled because of the fuel crisis and there's no room on our ten forty-five flight."

Naturally I reached for my airline guide and discovered that Western Airlines had an 11:20 flight from Phoenix to Seattle with three stops—San Diego, Los Angeles and San Francisco. It was our only hope. We managed to get space on all legs except the twenty-five minute hop between San Diego and Los Angeles. However, the reservation clerk indicated that the flight from San Diego to Los Angeles usually had a lot of no-shows and suggested that we make a standby reservation, which we did.

Now we had about two and one-half hours to kill before our flight, so we went back to American Airlines and rechecked the progress of our original flight. The ticket agent said it would be leaving at about 10:30 for Los Angeles. Hmmm. Jim and I decided that we'd take the American flight to L.A. and then change to the Western flight to San Francisco and Seattle, thus averting the possibility of not getting a seat on Western from San Diego to Los Angeles. So the American agent took our names and promised to page us before he boarded passengers for the flight to Los Angeles.

Jim and I strolled out to the lobby, and while we were standing there I happened to glance at a television set that displays flight departures and arrivals. I laughed. The TV said our flight to L.A. was leaving at 9:10. Hell, it was 9:08 now and just five minutes ago the agent had told us the flight would not be leaving until 10:30. Then I stopped laughing. "Let's go," I said to Capers, and we both started to run for the boarding area. When we got there, our plane to Los Angeles was taxiing from the gate and rolling toward the runway.

No, I wasn't mad. I was madder than mad. However, age and maturity showed. I said, "I'll be double dipped in cement" only eight times and I smashed my right hand against the counter only five times. If American had pulled this stunt on me three years ago, I'd have been heard down in Tucson.

So, instead of reaching our hotel in Seattle around 11:00 A.M., we didn't even leave Phoenix until 11:20 A.M. Fortunately, space did open up on the San Diego to Los Angeles leg, and we eventually arrived in Seattle around 5:00 P.M. Cripes, all things considered, we had been up for twelve hours and our real work had not even begun yet. And another thing: I'll be working in my third time zone in three nights. My body still feels as though it's back in Detroit, while my mind is somewhere between Phoenix and Seattle. I hope they both make it to the game tonight.

Like all officials, I am not a great admirer of the Coliseum in Seattle where the SuperSonics play their games because of the fact that the visiting team and the officials must walk the same 100-yard tunnel to get to their respective dressing rooms both at halftime and at the conclusion of the game. As you might suspect, this situation has presented real problems for officials in the past and will continue to create trouble until the NBA orders the Seattle team to provide a separate dressing room for the referees away from the quarters used by the competing teams. The referees call that tunnel "The Last Mile," and it has been the scene of some of the most heated debates ever conducted in the NBA.

I particularly remember a vicious name-calling and finger-waving session I had in that tunnel one night with Jack Ramsay, who was coaching the 76ers at the time. Manny Sokol was my officiating partner, and with two seconds left in the game Philadelphia missed a potential game-winning shot and the ball went out of bounds. Manny properly gave the ball to Seattle's Bob Rule under the basket, and all Rule had to do was flip it to Lenny Wilkens, who was standing alone about five feet from Rule, and let the clock run out. Unbelievably, Rule ignored Wilkens and fired the ball down court, hoping to hit a teammate for an easy basket. Slam! The ball hit the overhead clock. So now Philadelphia—trailing by one point—got the ball at midcourt, still with two seconds to play.

The 76ers called time out and set up a play for Billy Cunningham, their best shooter. Hal Greer took the ball at the sidelines and looked for Cunningham, but Cunningham couldn't get away from Rule. In desperation Greer finally threw the ball toward Cunningham, but Rule—reacting to the broken play—reached out and knocked the ball away. Once Rule touched the ball, of course, the clock was activated—and the game ended with the ball rolling across the court. Meanwhile, Cunningham was stretched out on the floor, pounding his fists and kicking his feet.

Listen. Billy Cunningham is the most verbally agressive player I have ever encountered in the NBA. He baits the referees every second he's on the court, and he goes overboard with the histrionics. He is the original actor—besides being a great player. Cunningham never gets vicious with his complaints. He's just a complainer, and he accepts technical fouls the same way he accepts Monday following Sunday. On this play, though, Cunningham was protesting that Rule had fouled him. I thought Billy was carrying his protests too far, so I called a technical on him. Meanwhile, Ramsay, who also felt that Cunningham had been fouled, was all over Manny Sokol.

Playing peacemaker, I stepped between Sokol and Ramsay and tried to get them to cut the dialogue. Instead, Ramsay and I conducted a raging debate for the entire length of the tunnel. Manny and I finally reached our dressing room, but before we even had a chance to sit down Ramsay was back pounding on the door. I opened the door and looked Ramsay in the eye. "Sir," I said, "it would be an exercise in futility for you should you and I ever engage in fisticuffs." Ramsay stepped back, stunned. And so were the half-dozen reporters standing in the corridor. I slammed the door on all of them.

The Seattle-Cleveland game was a relatively timid affair,

with Seattle winning big. I called a technical on Cavaliers Coach Bill Fitch early in the game when he yelled "Bullshit!" after I called a two-shot foul on a Cavalier who had hacked Spencer Haywood in the act of shooting. Later in the game I had to monitor a minor dispute between Lenny Wilkens, who used to coach the SuperSonics and now plays for the Cavaliers, and Milt Williams, one of the Seattle guards. Bill Russell has been teaching the concept of an all-court, team-style defense to the SuperSonics, and Williams was following instructions to the letter. In fact, Williams played Wilkens so closely that he even followed Lenny to the Cleveland bench during a time out. On this one play I had the ball at mid-court and was ready to give it to Austin Carr of the Cavaliers. Suddenly, Wilkens and Williams started at each other for about the tenth time. "Gentlemen," I said, "cut it out. The ball is not in play. Wait until I give it to Mr. Carr, then you can resume banging heads." My words seemed to calm tempers; Wilkens and Williams played the rest of the game without incident.

Part of a referee's job should be preventive. We don't always have to be punitive. But we must control the game. How? Any way we can. For instance, say that you and I are having a ditch-digging contest. I might dig with my left hand on the bottom of the shovel, you might dig with your right hand on the bottom. I might pile my dirt to the right of the ditch, you might pile yours to the left. My pile might be neat, yours might be splattered all over the place. Who cares? As long as the hole gets dug to the specifications of the job, that's all that matters. Well, that's officiating, too.

And another thing. I always tell young officials in the NBA that they ought to use polysyllabic words whenever possible during their debates with players and coaches. Polysyllabic words not only command prompt attention but, in the heat of moment, can often leave people speechless.

Saturday, November 17 (Philadelphia at Golden State)

Catch this scene at the Seattle airport. I was standing near the payphone in the boarding area after checking-in for the flight to Oakland when the man next to me picked up the phone, deposited a dime, dialed a number and asked if he was speaking to the "cat disposal service." I wasn't eavesdropping, mind you, because the man was only two feet away. However, I'm an animal lover, and his question fascinated me.

Then he said: "Do you have a group rate?"

After a short pause, he said: "How much does it cost?"

Well, I was laughing hysterically, and the other passengers in the boarding area were giving me funny looks. I went over to Jim Capers, who was giving me a funny look too, told him what the man had said, and Capers burst out laughing.

A few minutes later the man on the phone walked by and I couldn't resist telling him that I had overheard his conversation with the cat disposal service. He explained that some friends had left their cat with him, and a couple of days later the cat produced a litter of six kittens. The man was panicking because his wife, who was at home sitting with the cat and her kittens, told him she'd leave him forever if the cats weren't out of the house by Monday morning. So he called the humane society to get a group disposal rate. At least that's what he *said*.

We made Oakland without complications, thank God, and I spent the afternoon catching up on my rest. In the game the 76ers upset the Warriors, who had to play without Cazzie Russell. I saw Cazzie before the game and his face was so contorted with pain that I figured he must have reinjured his back, only to learn that he just had an upset stomach. I told him never to recommend any restaurants to me. Philadelphia has really improved under Shue's patient coaching. However, late in the game, as the lead bounced back and forth, Shue no doubt got some more gray hairs as his young team fought to maintain its court composure.

On one play a Philadelphia guard stole the ball, whipped it down court to Steve Mix, who was standing all alone under the basket, and then—as fate would have it—Mix missed the layup. No problem. The same Philadelphia guard re-stole the ball, fired it back to Mix and this time Mix bounced the ball off the rim as he tried to slam-dunk it through the basket. I happened to look over at Shue as the ball caromed out of bounds, and Gene's chin was down around his ankles. Mix was absolutely disconsolate. He has bounced around NBA benches for several years, and spent last season playing in a weekend pro league somewhere in the Midwest. Now he has developed into a strong and solid forward with about a 15-point-per-game scoring average. I hope he doesn't let things like this bother him—he missed two easy baskets, but his team won anyway. So forget it.

I suppose that's easy for a referee to say because referees never miss baskets.

Sunday, November 18 (Cleveland at Los Angeles)

It's supposed to be a surprise, but I understand that they will stop the Lakers-Cavaliers game on the first whistle tonight and give me the game ball. Believe me, that's not what I usually get on the first whistle. Seventeen years ago I hoped that I'd be able to survive three or four years as a referee in the NBA. And now tonight here in the Forum I will referee the 1,000th game of my NBA career. One thousand games! I can't believe it. I just pray the first whistle is an innocent call, something like an out-of-bounds pass or a kicked ball. With my luck, though, I'll probably blow the first whistle and call one of the Lakers for goal-tending.

I still remember my first regular-season game in the NBA when I worked with Mendy Rudolph at the Onondaga War Memorial Auditorium in Syracuse. I was a cocky kid from the Bronx, and Mendy was the experienced professional. The Auditorium has a stage at one end, and our dressing room was down past several rows of seats and behind a curtain. When we stepped from behind the curtain and began to walk down the steps from the stage, we were greeted with a chorus of shouts and boos. I figured they must have been for Mendy because the people in Syracuse didn't know Richie Powers from a Dewar's bottle. As we walked toward the court, Mendy said: "Hear that, Richie?" I nodded. "Well, when you hear them booing you, consider that you've got it made." Three weeks later I got that same booing treatment from the friendly people in Syracuse.

I remember a ten-game exhibition barnstorming tour through New England that I made with Red Auerbach's Celtics and the Cincinnati Royals back in 1957, just before the start of my rookie year. One morning I woke up in a hotel room in Booth Bay Harbor, Maine, walked over to the only window in the room and pulled up the shade. As I looked out the window, I noticed a man on the same floor of the building across the street waving at me very animatedly. I waved back at him. Friendly people they have here in Maine, I thought. Then it struck me. There were bars across the window of the man's room. He was in jail.

We left Booth Bay Harbor for an exhibition in Houlton, Maine, and after the game I had my first live encounter session with Mr. Auerbach. I was standing in the hotel lobby, waiting for Jim Gaffney, my officiating partner, to join me for a couple of drinks, and suddenly there was Auerbach asking me if I had a minute to talk with him. Imagine that? I said, "Yes, sir"—and not condescendingly, either. I still call Auerbach "Sir" because of the great respect I have for the man. He said to me, "Rich, I want to give you two pieces of advice if I can." I nodded my head.

"First of all, you have a tendency to turn your head and start down the floor immediately after calling a foul. As a result, you lose sight of the ball." I told Auerbach that I was aware of the problem; that Charlie Eckman, an excellent official who later coached several NBA teams, had warned me of the consequences already; and that I was working to correct it. Auerbach said, "You'd better work harder on it because we're quick in this league and a team could steal the ball while you're looking the wrong way. Then you've lost the play, and maybe you'll end up in a war."

At that time in the NBA, a coach had the prerogative to call time out, gesture the referee to his side and then discuss an officiating decision without fear of penalty. Red knew that I would be facing such a predicament with him in my career, probably within a week or two, since the NBA season was opening in a matter of days, so he also gave me some avuncular counsel. "The rule, as you know, specifies that I can call you over to my bench at any time," Auerbach said. "When I call you over, let me say what I have to say —even if it sounds ridiculous—because I'm doing it for a purpose. Then when I finish, give me your answer and walk away. After that my actions will decide whether *you* will give me a technical foul, an ejection—or nothing. But at least you've given me the courtesy of listening to me."

Over the years I ejected Auerbach from some games, and I gave him several technical fouls. However, I always listened to him first. I probably was unfair to him on occasion, but 99 percent of the time Mr. Auerbach got what he deserved. Of course, oftentimes an ejection or a technical foul was part of Red's plan to motivate his players. Whatever he did, it usually worked.

I also learned early in my NBA career that a referee should never threaten players with a technical foul or an ejection. The referee should *promise* them a technical foul or an ejection. I always do what I say I'm going to do on the court. If I don't, if I hedge slightly and decide to give a player another chance, then I've lost control of the game. And that's the absolute worst thing that can happen to an official in any sport.

In one of my first NBA games I called a foul on Jungle Jim Loscutoff of the Celtics. Loscutoff was a muscular forward who intimidated players with his mere presence on the court. Some people called him a hatchetman, but I always thought he was a gentle giant. I never saw him start a fight or throw a punch, although I guess he did both on occasion. After signaling this foul on Loscutoff, I started to move around him and happened to bump into his arm. "Excuse me," I said. Two minutes later I called another foul on him. I started to go around him again and, sure enough, I bumped into his arm. This time, though, he had moved his arm so that I had to bump into it. "Excuse me," I said. And then, quietly, I told Loscutoff that if I ran into his arm again I would eject him from the game. Well, two minutes later I called another foul on Loscutoff, and ran into his arm for the third time.

"You're gone," I said to Loscutoff, and he left without an argument.

On the Celtics bench, though, Auerbach was redder than usual.

"Richie, what the hell's going on?" he yelled at me.

"Speak to Loscutoff at the half," I said.

Thinking about Loscutoff, the funniest thing I've ever seen in basketball was a non-fight between Jungle Jim and little Guy Rodgers of the old Philadelphia Warriors in the closing seconds of a quiet game in the early 1960s. The players were standing at center court, waiting for a jump ball, when Rodgers suddenly walked up, hauled off and smacked Loscutoff behind the left ear with a punch. What possessed Rodgers to hit Loscutoff I'll never know. Guy was no bigger than 6 feet 1 inch and weighed only about 185 pounds. Jungle Jim was 6 feet 6 inches and 230 pounds of muscle. Loscutoff reached up and grabbed his left ear, then turned around and saw Rodgers, who now wore the look of a man who realized that doom was near.

Rodgers promptly took off at full speed and started to run to his right. Ooops. He was running toward the Boston bench. He stopped, turned left and ran down the end line of the court with Loscutoff in hot pursuit. Picture this.

There were ten men in the center of the court—the eight players and the two referees—watching the great chase, doubled over with laughter. For some reason, Loscutoff never tried to head Rodgers off on the court. The two players simply ran around the perimeter of the court, until Rodgers spun toward an exit and galloped to the Philadelphia dressing room. Listen. I don't want to think what would have happened if Jungle Jim had ever caught Rodgers that night.

My greatest game—or, rather, the greatest game I've ever had the privilege to referee—was my first championship contest: Game Seven of the great Boston–Los Angeles series in 1962, my fifth year in the league. I was scheduled to be the alternate official behind Sid Borgia and Mendy Rudolph. However, on the flight from New York to Boston, Borgia told me that Rudolph did not want to work the seventh game because it was Passover and that I would be the second official. I'll never forget that night in the Boston Garden.

Before the game Fred Schaus, the coach of the Lakers, did a strange thing: he requested a meeting of the coaches and the officials at center court. As we stood around in a circle, Schaus said to Sid and me: "Are you people going to work this game any differently?" Borgia was absolutely stunned by Schaus' comment. He said nothing. He just stared at Schaus. I did the talking. "I don't see anything different about this game except that maybe it's the most important game of the year—for you," I said flatly and then walked away.

The Celtics and Lakers matched baskets all night, and the score was tied in the closing seconds of regulation time. Boston had the ball, and Frank Ramsey drove down the lane for what could have been the go-ahead basket. Borgia, though, made a gutty call and hit Ramsey with a charging foul. There were 13,909 people packed into the Boston Garden, and Sid didn't have a friend in the house. So the Lakers got the ball and carefully stalled for the last shot.

They finally maneuvered Frank Selvy to an open spot about ten-feet from the basket on the left—and with three seconds left to play Selvy took his shot. If he made it, the Boston dynasty—four world championships in five years—was dead. The ball hit the far side of the rim, bounced into the air, hit the near side of the rim and dropped into Bill Russell's hands. No basket. And the game went into overtime.

Poor Elgin Baylor. As Selvy's shot bounced around the rim, Baylor leaped into the air and seemed ready to tip the ball through the basket. According to the rules in those days, an offensive player such as Baylor *could* touch the ball when it was above the rim. Suddenly, though, Baylor pulled his hands back. Why? That was the question everyone asked after the game. Well, earlier that season Baylor faced practically the same situation in a game against the St. Louis Hawks and tipped the ball through the basket *after* the game-ending buzzer had gone off. What upset him was that the ball definitely was going through the basket anyway. By touching it, of course, Baylor had nullified the basket. He obviously was afraid that he would do the same thing on Selvy's shot, too.

The Celtics won the game—and the championship—in the overtime. As Borgia and I left the court, Sid said to me, "Rich, if Selvy's shot had gone in after that charging call against Ramsey, they might have buried us here at center court." True.

Well, it's nap time. I'm trying to forget I will be working my fifth game in five nights, and that tomorrow at 7:00 A.M. I will be 3,000 miles away from here in Greenwich. Getaway games are a problem for all referees because we tend to think about what we will be doing tomorrow at home—and not tonight on the court. These are games when mental lassitude can create big problems.

I blew the first whistle of the game after exactly 10 seconds of play. Johnny Nucatola calls me the "King of the Offensive Fouls," so he will be happy to know that I called an offensive foul—not on one of the Lakers but on Austin Carr of the Cavaliers. Once I blew the whistle, Chick Hearn, the radio and television voice of the Lakers, took the P.A. microphone and announced to the crowd that this was my 1,000th game. At the same time Pete Newell, the L.A. General Manager, walked onto the court and gave me the game ball. Then Bill Fitch, the witty coach of the Cavaliers, handed me one of those mini-basketballs and said: "This is a Cleveland basketball." On it someone had written: "To the man who has flown more miles than the Red Baron." I received a standing ovation from the great capacity crowd at the Forum, the first standing-o of my career.

In the game the Lakers beat the Cavaliers despite the absence of Jerry West and Bill Bridges from their lineup. West now has pneumonia, or so the doctors think. Elmore Smith, the seven-foot center the Lakers acquired from Buffalo to replace Wilt Chamberlain, blocked about two dozen Cleveland shots, almost all of them from inside the free-throw line. By my figuring, Smith saved 20 points for the Lakers, and since they won by only 2 points, Smith won the game for them.

Afterwards I took my game ball to both dressing rooms and had the players and coaches autograph it. Then to the airport to catch the red-eye special back to New York. My eyes may get a little redder than usual, too, because I plan to celebrate this milestone with a few extra Double Ds. (Or maybe they'll have some champagne onboard.)

Friday, November 23 (Phoenix at Chicago)

I had an interesting thought—yes, even referees have interesting thoughts at times—while flying from New York to Chicago this morning after spending a four-day mini-vacation in Greenwich with the family. By my figuring, I run about six miles a game, so that means I've run about 6,000 miles on basketball courts the last seventeen years.

Cripes! I've run back and forth across the United States! I must admit in all candor, though, that I don't think I could run from Park Avenue to Madison Avenue—a distance of one city block—without stopping to catch my breath halfway down the street.

Phoenix won its first road game of the season, beating the Bulls by several points. As generally happens in close games, the most suspenseful action occurred during the final minute, and, as luck would have it, I played a major role in the developments. On one play Phoenix was leading by a basket and facing a Chicago all-court press when the ball was passed in from mid-court to Charlie Scott at the center jump circle in the last minute of play. When Scott took the ball, Norm Van Lier of the Bulls reached out and tried to slap it away, and in so doing, crashed against Scott's shoulder. I promptly, and properly, called a foul. Van Lier protested vigorously, but the foul was there. Sometimes players don't realize they have hit another player because they lose themselves in the heat of the competition. Scott converted the two free throws to give Phoenix a 4-point lead.

Chicago came down court quickly and scored immediately, reducing Phoenix' lead to 2 points. On the in-bounds play, the Bulls stole the ball and tried to set up Chet Walker for the tying basket. But as Walker drove for the hoop he stumbled and crashed into a defensive player. I immediately called a charging foul on Walker, much to the angry amazement of all the Bulls, who felt I should have called a foul on the defensive player.

After the game I let a few Chicago reporters come into our dressing room. In games where the outcome has been directly affected by a referee's decision in the final moments, reporters frequently request permission to interview the officials afterwards. The NBA, unlike the other major sports, wants its officials to communicate with the press and explain the thinking and the rules behind a decision. One of the writers—Lacey Banks—asked me if there

(49)

was any difference between an early and a late foul. I said: "When a foul is there, you must call it—regardless of the score or the time. We get paid to call fouls for forty-eight minutes—and longer if there's an overtime." The reporter kept nodding his head as he scribbled my answer. "Listen," I said to him, "if I miss a call after forty-seven minutes and thirty seconds of a game, I may ruin the game completely. Hillary reached the top of Mt. Everest. If he had stopped ten-feet short, well, who'd remember Hillary? In basketball the referees can't stop even one-second short."

Near the end of the game I also had to silence the Chicago public-address announcer. Each time the Bulls scored a basket this man waved his arms and cheered noisily, and each time the Suns scored this man yelled at the referees. Finally I went over to him during a time out and said: "Listen, I know you're a fan, but you can't behave like a fan because you're sitting here in an official capacity. If you want to cheerlead, go sit in the stands." "I'm sorry," he said. "I'll try to be more professional." "You'd better," I said, "or else I'll put some tape over your mouth and tie your arms to the chair."

Paul Mihalak, who is working the CBS-TV game here tomorrow, attended the game as an observer. We had dinner afterward at the Steak House behind the Pick-Congress Hotel, and I asked Paul for his comments. I find that referees usually are very open with each other. In fact, I demand openness. If I mishandle a play, I want my officiating partner or an official in the stands to tell me what I did wrong. No one is perfect. Well, Paul noted, on one play I had called a foul on Jerry Sloan of the Bulls for banging into Charlie Scott, and Paul—looking at the play from another angle—thought I should have called the foul on Scott. We discussed the play for about twenty minutes, and maybe Paul was right. I'm going to check with the league office and see if Johnny Nucatola can get the films of the game so that I can inspect them with regard to the Sloan-Scott incident.

Paul laughed about something that happened in a Chicago game that he worked with Tommy Nunez, a rookie official. Nunez called a technical foul on one of the coaches. Incensed, the coach questioned Nunez about his nationality. "Mexicano!" Tommy said. "What made you want to become a referee?" the coach asked. Nunez retorted, "It's a helluva lot better than chopping lettuce!" End of discussion.

Sunday, November 25 (New York at Capital)

I didn't understand why the shuttle flight from New York to Washington was so bumpy, and why so many passengers were using their "barf bags." Then I got into my rental car, turned on the radio and heard that a tornado warning was in effect for the entire Washington area.

The Bullets will be moving into the new Capital Centre in Largo, Maryland, next week, so today's Bullets-Knicks game will be the last NBA contest played in Cole Field House on the University of Maryland campus. I'm sure that NBA players and officials everywhere are glad for that. For one thing, the rims and the backboards in the fieldhouse are too hard and springy, and don't accept the ball very well. In fact, the ball tends to carom off and dart toward rebounders. What we should use today is a less-inflated ball, but rules are rules.

Baskets. Listen, referees pray for baskets. In fact, we probably pray for them more fervently than the player who shoots the ball. I hate rebounding plays. Once the ball goes through the hoop, the play stops. But a rebound means continuous action and more physical contact, and more fouls.

The second reason I don't like the fieldhouse is because the hardwood floor is laid directly over concrete and has no give or spring, unlike the portable floors used in most buildings. The floor probably will last forever, but it sure is tough on players. And referees. I don't think any athlete could survive more than three or four years of regular play on such a surface. They had the same problem in Atlanta when the Hawks had to play at the Georgia Tech Fieldhouse while the Omni was being constructed, and Bill Bridges once told me that playing there regularly took at least two years from his active career.

Sure enough, Willis Reed injured his knee again tonight and limped off the floor. I suspect that the hardwood floor contributed to the injury, even though Willis' knees are already badly injured. However, before he left Reed prevented a major altercation when he stepped between his teammate Phil Jackson and referee Forrest Harris. Harris had called Jackson for his sixth—and eliminating—foul of the game, and the call so irked Jackson that he swore at Harris, thus earning a technical foul. Then the technical so irked Jackson that it appeared for a moment that he would physically attack Harris. Which is when Reed intervened, thank God.

Late in the game, with the Bullets running the Knicks off the court, I had my own problems. I called a foul on one of the Knicks, and Red Holzman yelled: "Goddammit, you always get the second one!" implying I had missed an earlier infraction against a Bullet player. Still angry, Holzman appended his remark: "You're horseshit!" Technical foul on Holzman. The announcement was made over the p.a. system and the crowd reacted loudly. I could see Holzman shouting in my direction but as I couldn't hear him in all the hubbub I asked him what he had just said. "You're horseshit!" he stormed. I signaled for another technical foul and ordered him from the premises.

According to the rules, no one except the captains can talk to an official during a game, and the captain can talk to us only during a time out called by his team. And even then he can only discuss the rules. Of course, we tend to accept general conversation from players and coaches because of the nature of the game. In basketball, the referees will give the players and coaches a second chance—except, of course, when they say the magic word. By giving them a second chance, we tell them: "Okay, you've broken the rules and now control yourself or you're gone."

I don't really know what Holzman was trying to prove by calling me horseshit. I do remember that last year I ejected Holzman in Oakland when the Knicks were trailing by 17 points, and after his eviction they rallied to win. Maybe he uses his outbursts against the referees as a psychological weapon on his players.

Nevertheless, after I ejected Holzman, the game became very rough. In fact, I even told a Knick to "play basketball, not football" during a rebounding melee, trying to prevent something before it happened. At the end, though, the Bullets and the Knicks really were playing football. In fact, Forrest and I must have called at least fifteen personal fouls during the last four minutes—about one every fifteen seconds. I even called a foul that could have passed for clipping, something I had never seen before on a basketball floor.

After the game Wes Unseld of the Bullets congratulated me on my 1,000th game, and on the shuttle back to New York Walt Frazier of the Knicks stopped by and congratulated me, too. I was stunned. It was the first time Clyde had ever spoken to me off the floor—and the first time I heard him say anything other than "hello."

I had a somewhat longer conversation on the plane with Bill Bradley. I told Bill that Willis Reed and Wes Unseld were truly courageous to play with the cumbersome encasements strapped to their injured knees, knowing that the slightest bump or twist might send them to the sidelines forever. "It's not just that," Bradley said. "What you don't see, and what the fans never see, is the time that they spend before and after the game limping around in unbelievable pain. They keep ice on their knees for at least an hour before and after each game. They're incredible athletes, that's all."

Per custom, I called the league office in New York and reported the incidents that had happened during last night's game, particularly the Jackson and Holzman ejections. Later in the morning the office called back to say that Holzman contended I had "not walked away from the scene of the crime" and had, in effect, baited him into swearing at me the second time. I was ordered to report to the office immediately and discuss the situation with Johnny Nucatola, who hears and moderates all complaints about the referees. I took the train into New York and cabbed across town to No. 2 Penn Plaza. The NBA's executive suites are on the 20th floor—and they happen to overlook Madison Square Garden, home, of course, of the Knicks.

It's never a nice feeling to get called on the carpet, but Nucatola—a former referee himself—usually is understanding and quite sympathetic to the plight of the officials. Our discussion centered not so much on the reasons for my ejection of Holzman but on the fact that I did indeed invite him to repeat his statement the second time. I imagine that if I had turned my back on Holzman and walked away the ejection would never have occurred. However, in all good conscience, I knew I had not intended to bait him. Still, I will not do it again. There are two sides to every dispute. One side cannot be totally in the right. In this situation both Holzman *and* Powers were at fault. Although as far as I know, referees don't run around telling coaches they are horseshit.

The Holzman case reminds me of a playoff game in Los Angeles years ago when I threw my whistle at Celtics Coach Red Auerbach in response to his repeated assertions that I was not only a no-good referee but a few things worse to boot. It began when I called a foul on Tommy Heinsohn on an out-of-bounds play. Heinsohn got mad at the call, claiming I was not in position to call the play. He tossed a few deleted expletives in my direction, so I deleted him

(54)

from the game. At the half Auerbach asked me what Hein-sohn had said, so I told him. Red agreed I had done the right thing. But he also said I had not been in position to call the play correctly.

In the second half Auerbach kept blasting away, and pretty strongly, too. Then, during a time out, he really cut loose with the polysyllabics. I had my whistle in my right hand, as always. I turned and stared at Auerbach and then, with a complete lack of cool, flipped the whistle at him. It landed on the floor and skidded between his legs. Christ, was I mad! I went over to pick up the whistle and said: "You guys don't deserve good referees!"

After the game I returned to the Statler-Hilton Hotel, downed a couple of Double Ds and went to bed. However, I couldn't get to sleep, so I went downstairs and bought the early editions of the L.A. newspapers. There, in living black-and-white, right at the top of the first page of the sports section, was a quote from a Boston player who natu-rally preferred to remain anonymous: "Powers was so far from the play on Heinsohn's foul that he was sitting in a certain movie star's lap." I exploded. I wasn't anywhere near any movie star. I was in the middle of the court, right where I should have been.

That was it. Enough was enough. I decided to retire at the end of the playoffs. Let them find some other whipping boy.

As it developed, I was scheduled to work the next Bos-ton–Los Angeles playoff game. Before the opening tap Auerbach walked over and apologized for his actions dur-ing the last game. He said he was wrong, that the game films had proved I made the proper call on Heinsohn. Once again Auerbach had displayed his class, admitting that he made a mistake. "Thank you, Red," I said. "But I'm afraid you're a little late. I couldn't sleep after that game and I've decided to quit." Later that night he asked me if I had meant what I had said. "Yes," I said flatly. And I did quit. That was my first retirement.

I stayed away from basketball for a year and sold advertising space for *Steel Magazine*—not *Steal Magazine*. But I missed the game and the involvement; in fact, I couldn't even watch games at the Garden or on television because I always ended up being an armchair referee. It was a stupid retirement, done in a fit of pique and in a display of supreme immaturity. I unretired the following year.

For the next two seasons, 1966 through 1968, I combined the full-time careers of an NBA referee and an advertising space salesman. Then, before the start of the 1968–69 season, Dolph Schayes, then the supervisor of officials, informed me that the league wanted only full-time referees and, therefore, no longer needed the services of Richie Powers the advertising salesman. Okay.

However, in the summer of 1969 four experienced NBA officials—Joe Gushue, John Vanak, Earl Strom and Norm Drucker—jumped to the fledgling American Basketball Association. When I read about their defection, I immediately called Mendy Rudolph, who was referee-in-chief, and asked if he could use my services. "No," he said flatly. "We're going with what we have." Shortly thereafter the ABA contacted me and asked if I was interested in returning to basketball. I jumped at the chance and accepted an offer to work as an ABA referee.

I weighed that decision for a week and did an abrupt about-face. If I was going to referee again, I was going to do it in the NBA. And only the NBA. So I contacted Walter Kennedy, the president of the NBA, and offered my services. On a full-time basis. We made a handshake agreement, and I worked full-time for five months of the season. Then the league hired me to work the playoffs, and, in fact, I worked the final game of the championship series when the Knicks beat the Lakers in New York. I was back—for good.

Usually I never lose my cool the way I did with Holzman and Auerbach. I try to use my temper, not lose it. I remember watching Nikita Khruschev's shoe-pounding exhibition on television with my father, and remarking that Khruschev must be out of his mind to be acting like that. My father just looked at me and laughed. "Rich," he said, "Mr. Khruschev's pulling an old trick. He's not losing his temper, he's using it. Don't you think the people at the U.N. are getting the message that the Russians aren't very happy?"

Friday, November 30 (Boston at Milwaukee)

When the Celtics and the Bucks get together for a shoot-out, the games begin to resemble the Indianapolis 500. Tonight's game was so wide-open, so fast and so furious, that I was reminded of the days when I worked for Monsignor Mooney at the Joseph Kennedy Memorial Center in Harlem. The kids there ran so much that each referee worked only one end of the floor in order to preserve his legs for another day.

The Celtics and the Bucks averaged a shot every six or seven seconds for the first three quarters. Unfortunately, neither team shot very well, so there was a lot of rebounding. Fortunately, the rebounding was unusually clean, and once a team missed a shot, the ball promptly headed off in the other direction without incident. There was never anything even close to a 24-second violation, and during one time out I kidded the operator of the 24-second clock that he was getting a paid vacation. "Are you serious?" he grumbled. "My arm is about ready to fall off."

The Bucks, with Oscar Robertson playing 45 minutes and dominating the action, chased the Celtics off the Milwaukee court, rallying from an early 10-point deficit to win by more than 20. I guess the most enjoyable part of a Milwaukee-Boston game is watching the battle between Kareem Abdul-Jabbar and Dave Cowens. They ask no quarter —and give none. Better yet, they never bitch to the referees about anything. Jabbar is about six inches taller than Cowens, but Cowens manages to give Jabbar more problems than any other center in the league. Unlike most centers, Cowens can hit consistently with jump shots from the twenty-foot range. Thus, he forces Jabbar to abandon his preferred defensive position around the basket and makes him move in unfamiliar circles. Cowens is the fastest 6-foot–9-inch man in captivity and, like his teammate John Havlicek, never seems to get tired.

After the game I met Alan Brunkhorst, who recently retired as an NBA official, back at the motel. Alan is taking his real-estate examination tomorrow. Old NBA referees don't lose their whistles, they just become real-estate salesmen, I guess. I told Alan I'd be glad to refer him to any of my friends who might be moving to Milwaukee, and he said he'd refer his New York–bound friends to me. Now if the biggest company in Milwaukee decides to move lock, stock and barrel to New York, I may be able to get ten or fifteen commissions.

Saturday, December 1 (Cleveland at New York)

I can't recall the last time I was so uptight about a basketball game. It's the Knicks, who have lost five straight, against the Cavaliers, who have lost three straight, at Madison Square Garden, but what bothers me is that it might become Holzman against Powers before the night is over. This will be our first chance to exchange pleasantries—at least I hope they're pleasantries—since last week's episode in Maryland.

Johnny Nucatola suspected I'd be tense, so he dropped into the dressing room before the game to try and get my mind off the upcoming confrontation. He told me the story of a referee who asked him if it was all right to shave at halftime. "Why?" Nucatola asked. "Well, when I'm freshly shaved my face tingles and I seem to get up more for the second half." Unbelievable.

The game bombed out early, with the Knicks rolling to

a 20-point lead and maintaining it throughout. In the late stages both teams sent their subs onto the court, and, as always, the game deteriorated into a roller-derby as the players began to attack one another instead of the basket. And then came the incident that I will never forget, or be allowed to forget, because I'm sure people will be kidding me about it for years.

Jim Cleamons of the Cavaliers kept shooting and missing, and every time he missed he complained that someone had hit him. Cleamons was taking his shots from an isolation booth but was understandably upset with himself. On this particular play he was defending against Henry Bibby when the ball broke loose and began to roll away. They both went after it, in a tangle of arms and legs. Cleamons landed on his back, and Bibby careened out of bounds. I was about to call a double foul when I saw that Cleamons and Bibby were about to go after each other and start a general riot. So I ejected both of them for "fighting." Or wrestling. Or whatever. In the lexicon of the NBA, fighting can be construed as anything.

When I turned to give my decision to the scorer's table, I noticed that Bill Fitch, the Cleveland coach, was standing at center court. This was a flagrant violation, so I gave him a technical foul. Then Fitch had the audacity to insist that I had called him there. Listen, I don't call coaches anywhere, only captains, according to the rules.

Fitch was really upset. "You think Cleamons and Bibby were fighting?" he said. "Hell! My wife and I have better fights than that."

Ginger and I have had better fights than that, too.

Fitch refused to leave center court, so I told him that I was not going to waste any more time and proceeded to give him his second technical foul—and out he went. To his credit, he did not pursue the matter any longer. Then Holzman, in turn, asked me why I had ejected Bibby and Cleamons. "For fighting," I said. Holzman just laughed.

Play resumed after several explanatory conferences, and

on the next sequence of plays I saw Bob Rule of the Cavaliers push Hawthorne Wingo of the Knicks as Wingy drove for the basket. I immediately called a two-shot foul on Rule, and when I passed him en route to my position under the basket Rule stared down at me and said: "Where did I hit him?" I stared back at him. "Right in the back." Then Rule bent over, leveled his lips at my right ear, and yelled, "Bullshit!" The last syllable was barely out of his mouth when he was gone. See how things become compounded in a game?

However, I had controlled the game by sticking my neck in the meatgrinder—first ejecting Bibby and Cleamons, then Fitch, then Rule—and no doubt preventing something that we all would have been sorry for afterward. You know, everytime there's a fight in a game, the coaches and fans say to the referee: "Why did you let it occur?" I wasn't going to let it occur here.

In the dressing room I talked with Nucatola, who was quite upset. Not at me. At the players. And at the coaches. He thinks they ought to be able to control themselves better than they do, and I agree. As we talked Tom "The Bomb" Barnwell, who looks after the officials at the Garden, knocked on the door and asked me if I wanted to let any reporters into the room. "Sure," I said. So they came in, grouped in a semicircle and just looked at me. Nobody said anything. For a moment I felt like Fred Waring standing on the podium in front of the Pennsylvanians. So I raised my hands and said, "All right, gentlemen, let's sing." That broke the tension in the room, and one of the writers asked me about the dual ejections of Bibby and Cleamons.

"The game was developing an overaggressive attitude," I said. "The athletes were playing the man, not the ball, and bodies were colliding. So it seemed propitious for me to take control and prevent fights."

"Why was Fitch ejected?" someone asked. "Two technicals constitute an ejection," I answered. "Fitch got the technicals for leaving his bench area and refusing to return."

"What about Rule?" another man said. "Purely profanity," I said.

Then I looked at them. "Gentlemen," I said, "to me the all-encompassing point about the technical fouls was that the game remained under control. I'll burn down a building to prevent a game from getting out of hand."

The reporters seemed to appreciate my position. Personally, unlike some other NBA officials, I think the press comes to our room after a game in an attempt to inform the people about what happened—not hurt the referees. I try to be as articulate and as precise as possible in order to get my side across to them. Many times I think the inability to express himself hurts an official. We must be able to be articulate about our business. And if we shun the press, we only hurt ourselves.

Sunday, December 2

Talking about polysyllabic words, it's quite obvious that I don't know enough of them. For the 1,346th straight week, the *New York Times* Sunday crossword puzzle whipped Richie Powers. I guess I'm not such a wordsmith after all.

Tuesday, December 4 (Houston at Milwaukee)

Thank God you don't have to shovel rain. It was pouring buckets when I left Greenwich at 5:30 with the Dawn Patrol, and it is raining like crazy here. I'm sure the Bucks will be surprised to see me tonight, because I refereed their last home game—the shoot-out with the Celtics —and we rarely work back-to-back home games. Why? The NBA has decided that to eliminate the possible carry-over of any prior anger with an official it will not assign the same referee to successive home games, barring unusual circumstances, such as travel or weather problems.

Johnny Egan, the Houston coach, was in top screaming form tonight, questioning my every decision from the opening tap. He yelled at 3-seconds, walking, foul, no foul, and practically everything else. During one Houston time out he spent a good forty-five seconds spewing forth his best in my direction. He was flagrantly violating the rules, because captains—and only captains—can talk to me during a time out, and I finally said, "John, I think it would behoove you to coach your team and let the referees do their own work."

This quieted him—for about two seconds. On the next play Oscar Robertson had the ball and faked Rudy Tomjanovich into the air. As Tomjanovich was returning to the ground, Oscar put his shoulder into him, sending Tomjanovich staggering backward, and went up for a jumper. Smart players like Robertson occasionally attempt to take advantage of the referee's position on the court by moving into a defensive player and drawing a foul. But I knew what Oscar was doing because the play was clearly in my sight. He was fouled, true, but he also did some fouling himself. In this case they both happened to be guilty—and innocent. So I waved no-foul and let the action continue.

The next thing I saw was Egan standing fifteen feet away from his bench, yelling in my direction. I couldn't hear him, but I suspect he was not lavishing words of praise on me. So I called a technical on Egan for leaving the area of his bench. He was really upset now and asked me what prompted the technical. I wanted to laugh, but I just said, "The technical was for leaving the bench and for the constant diatribe you have directed toward me."

"Cripes!" he said. "You're taking the game from our hands."

To be honest, I didn't know what the score was at the time, so I looked up at the board and saw that Milwaukee was leading 66 to 50. "John," I said, "you've got to be kidding."

One thing I have discovered over the years is that an aggressive anti-referee attitude by a coach seems to permeate his team, and, true to form, the Houston players tried to impress me with their verbiage for the rest of the game. Finally, I had had enough, so I silenced them with Speech No. 26: "Gentlemen, let's put the forensic society to retirement." Loosely translated: shut up—or else. I didn't say it in a jocular tone, either. Listen. I can't let a member of one team get away with too much dialogue or else the other team will be looking for the same privilege. And there are no privileged characters on a basketball floor.

I met Alan Brunkhorst after the game again. He said the real-estate exam was more difficult than he had expected. Alan's wife, Nancy, who is in real estate, was with him. "Considering the way the market has been going," she said, "maybe he ought to go back to refereeing."

Friday, December 7 (Atlanta at Boston)

One of the real treats of my season is a game in Boston followed by an off day. I am not working tomorrow, so Ginger drove to Boston with me; we'll combine some pleasure with my business at the Boston Garden. We are staying at a motel out in Wellesley, near the home of Bob and Pat Futoran, two of our closest friends. Bob and Pat will drive Ginger to the game at the Garden, and afterward we'll all go out for a quiet dinner and a couple of nightcaps. Unfortunately, the schedule rarely provides such therapeutic breaks in my nomadic wanderings, but when it does I really enjoy it.

The Celtics beat the Atlanta Hawks on John Havlicek's 3-point play in the final minute. Early in the game—in fact, after the very first foul that I called on the Hawks—Atlanta Coach Cotton Fitzsimmons mumbled something about my waistline. He said he couldn't understand how a referee could start the season in such great shape and then proceed to get out of shape as the season progressed. I have not added even one ounce to my frame since the first day of training camp, three months ago. Still, I was tempted to tell Fitzsimmons that I'd start to lose weight as soon as they make a low-calorie Dewar's.

Jim Capers and I had only one slight problem in the game. With three seconds left in the first half, Hambone Williams of the Celtics was bringing the ball up court against Pistol Pete Maravich, who was pressing Williams very closely. Pistol Pete must be taking karate lessons, because he's very determined on defense these days. He stole the ball from Williams and knocked it toward the sideline. He began to chase the ball, but Hambone moved to his right and—as Pistol Pete sped by—threw his body into Maravich, driving him off the court. I was behind the action, but saw everything. Maravich somehow managed to remain on his feet—if he had been knocked down or crashed into the press table, I would have ejected Williams for "deliberate attempt to injure," because the act was flagrant. I quickly moved toward Maravich, who looked ready to take off after Williams. "Stay there," I told him. "I'll handle it." I went over and put my arm around Williams, who was shaking his head. He said he thought Maravich had fouled him while he was stealing the ball, but he also admitted that he had lost his head. I called a foul on Hambone and had no problem after that. Things were well under control the rest of the way.

The Maravich incident reminds me of an altercation between Pistol Pete and Phil Chenier of the Bullets on opening night of the 1972–73 season. I don't know what started them, but they swapped nouns and adjectives and verbs and adverbs for a couple of minutes, and it looked as though we would have a Pier Six brawl any moment. I leaped between them and bumped Maravich away. I was in the middle now. Pete said something unprintable to

Chenier, and when Chenier responded by making a menacing gesture, Pistol Pete kicked him with his left leg, hitting Chenier on his right thigh. It was unbelievable! I had never seen one player kick another in all my life. I promptly called a technical foul on Maravich for unsportsmanlike conduct.

Sunday, December 9 (Detroit at K.C.–Omaha)

The strangest thing happened tonight. The Detroit Pistons beat the K.C.–Omaha Kings 86 to 80 and—would you believe?—also protested the game. Here's what happened.

Nate Williams of the Kings tried to slam-dunk a shot, but the ball bounced off the rim and headed toward the sideline. One of Nate's mates picked up the ball just before it reached that out-of-bounds stripe, but then the 24-second clock went off. So the Kings player—apparently trying to "tie" the clock—tried an impossible shot that fell well short of the basket and was grabbed by one of the Pistons. Meanwhile, there was confusion everywhere because of the 24-second horn. When Williams hit the rim with his slam-dunk, the Kings beat the clock, as such, and the clock should have returned to 24 seconds when Williams' teammate collected the loose ball near the sideline. Instead, the horn went off, so I blew my whistle.

Now I was temporarily hung up because the error had been made by someone not on the court: the operator of the 24-second clock. I discussed the situation with the operator, who admitted he had goofed. So I had to call a jump ball. Both captains—Dave Bing of the Pistons and Sam Lacey of the Kings—were upset, claiming their team should have the ball. Bing called time out and came over to rehash the play with me. Lacey joined Bing and said he'd like to listen.

"No way," I said. "It's Detroit's time out—not yours."

"But I'm the captain," Lacey protested.

(65)

"I don't care if you're the Pope," I said. "Get out of here."

I explained the problem to Bing, who was sympathetic, and then re-explained it to Lacey, who also was sympathetic. At halftime Ray Scott, the Pistons' coach, walked off the court with me and I explained my decision to him. No need to call Phil Johnson, the Kings' coach, because this was not an argument—just an explanation. As we were walking off, some fans began to chant: "Powers is a bum! Powers is a bum!" Scott looked down at me—he's at least a foot taller than me—and said: "Richie, has anyone ever called you anything except a bum?" I had to laugh. "No, Ray," I said, "it's an occupational hazard."

After the game Scott approached me again. "Richie," he said, "what do I do about a protest?" I was stunned. "Ray," I said, "you've got to be kidding. There can't be a protest, because you won the game. And even if you lost you couldn't protest because in the end any error was mine."

By the way, all NBA coaches, not just Scott, seem to think that when they use the word "protest," the referees get all shook up. No way. There is only one basis for an official protest in the NBA: an incorrect interpretation of a rule. You cannot protest—officially, that is—a judgment call made by a referee. Referees must be advised by the coach that he is protesting the game for an alleged misinterpretation of the rule; then the coach has forty-eight hours in which he must officially file his protest with the league office. In my long NBA career, the league has never upheld any protest about a decision I made in a game. In fact, I don't believe there has ever been an official protest filed against one of my decisions.

Back in the dressing room Jim Capers, my partner, was upset. He had called an offensive foul on a Kings player, who responded with a stream of epithets. Listening to the crude verbiage, Jim sort of half-smiled. Not in a laughing way, mind you, but in a manner that indicated to the player that he couldn't get to Capers that way. As this was going on, Phil Johnson, the new coach of the Kings now that Bob Cousy has resigned, yelled: "Stop laughing, this is serious business." Sure it is, Phil. And you ought to control the mouths of your players. What bothered Capers was that Johnson actually thought he was smiling about a serious breach of conduct.

Capers and I were waiting for a cab after the game and happened to be standing alongside the Detroit players, who were boarding their bus. John Mengelt did not make the trip to Omaha because of an injury, so there was only one white player—Chris Ford—on the Pistons roster for the game. This situation suddenly hit forward Don Addams. He looked at Ford and said: "If it weren't for you, we'd look like the Harlem Globetrotters."

Monday, December 10 (off-day)

The phone was ringing when I walked in the door. Someone named Tony Kornheiser of *Newsday,* the big Long Island daily, said he was calling to get my reaction to the "dump" story in the most recent issue of *Sports Illustrated.* According to the story, written by Bob Briner, a sports promoter who was once affiliated with the Dallas Chaparrals of the ABA, the Seattle SuperSonics players willfully conspired to lose a game last January in order to get coach Tom Nissalke fired. I told Kornheiser I wouldn't talk with him because he used the word "dump"; that I had not read the article myself; had no knowledge of the alleged incident; didn't know Tony Kornheiser from a whole in the ground; and never discuss league matters with a stranger. I told him to sit tight for now, that I'd call the NBA office and get back to him. Maybe.

I talked to Johnny Nucatola, who explained the details— the alleged details, that is—of the story. The *SI* story claimed that the referees in several Seattle games even knew the players planned to lose games on purpose in order to get Nissalke fired. Frankly, I've never seen what I'd consider to be even a questionable game in the NBA. If I ever do, I'll be the first one to point a finger. Nucatola also gave me permission to call Kornheiser back. Nissalke, after all, did get fired.

"Had you heard anything about dumping games?" Kornheiser asked me.

I said, "If I had heard anything, I would have reported it to the league office immediately."

End of interview.

I'm sure that John Joyce, the security chief for the NBA, will nail this matter down in a short period of time. If the comments made in the article prove to be frivolous, let's indict the man who wrote them. If they aren't frivolous, let the sword of justice fall where it may. And if any referee knew about something out of order and did not report it, let him be fired. Immediately. And don't let him ever officiate again.

You know, I'd love to have someone indict me publicly the way they are indicting the Seattle players. Ol' Double D would become an instant millionaire. I'm doing a radio talk-show in Greenwich tonight with Jim Senich, and I expect that most of the calls from listeners will center on the Seattle story. Great! I think I'll let a little fur fly in the other direction for a change.

Tuesday, December 11 (Los Angeles at Cleveland)

I'm sure he didn't mean anything personal, but before the captains' meeting tonight at center court Jerry West of the Lakers told me the funny story about a fat man in Los Angeles who no longer attended the basketball games because he weighed more than 400 pounds and couldn't squeeze himself into a seat. I laughed and pulled in my stomach. "Jerry," I said, "if I owned the Lakers I'd let the guy in free and plant him near a concessions stand."

Then I told West and Austin Carr, who was acting captain of the Cavaliers in the absence of the injured Lenny Wilkens, the story of a promotion that backfired last week on Pat Williams, the general manager of the Atlanta Hawks. Knowing that Bob Lanier of the Pistons wears size 22 shoes, Williams decided to have a "Big Foot" night for a Hawks-Pistons game. Anybody with size 13 shoes or bigger would be allowed into the Omni for half price. The one person who didn't think too much of Williams' promotion was Bob Lanier who was upset that Williams seemed to be making a joke about the size of his feet. So Lanier scored more than 40 points, grabbed every rebound in sight, blocked a dozen or so shots and personally destroyed the Hawks in the game.

After the captains' meeting I walked past the Cleveland bench. "Ah, there's Richie Powers," Coach Bill Fitch said with a smile. "He'll clean out a building faster than a Chinese fire drill." Fitch still doesn't appreciate the action I took in New York ten days ago when I ejected Jim Cleamons and Henry Bibby for their so-called fight, and him close behind them. Can't win them all.

Say what you want about the people who live in Cleveland, if nothing else they are certainly imaginative. Several young men walked past the Lakers bench carrying a sign that said: "Connie Hawkins Almost Italian." Connie was so amused that he stood up and saluted. He's now the Franco Harris of basketball.

The Lakers are in a mild slump, having lost three straight, but they quickly exploded to a 13-point lead over the Cavaliers at halftime. However, Jim Brewer—playing his best game as a pro—rallied the Cavaliers with some tremendous rebounding and strong inside shooting, and they closed to within 1 point after the third quarter. One of the problems with the old arena here is the chicken wire —or the spaghetti, as I call it—that holds up the backboard at the Euclid Avenue end of the building. How do I know it is the Euclid Avenue end? Euclid, remember, invented geometry, and I've hated the guy since high school. The spaghetti sticks out about two feet from the side of the backboard, and on this one play the Lakers contended that a Cleveland shot had hit the wire en route to the basket, thus nullifying the shot. I had thought the same thing, but when I looked up a second time I noticed that the spaghetti wasn't wiggling. So I allowed the basket.

The game remained close throughout the fourth quarter, and it eventually went into overtime before the Cavaliers squeeked through 101 to 100. Now think about this for a second: early in the game Jim Price of the Lakers was shooting a free throw, and as he released the ball Connie Hawkins walked away from the foul line. According to the rules, once the free throw shooter has the ball, no player can change his physical position at the foul lane until he shoots. If a teammate of the shooter moves his position, the foul shot—good or bad—is wiped out. If a rival of the shooter moves his position, the shooter gets another chance if his shot happens to miss. Well, Price's free throw dropped through the basket but the Lakers lost the point because Hawkins had moved. The point prevented them from winning the game in regulation time. No wonder coaches all get prematurely gray.

For me, the toughest part about handling Lakers games involves the broad and very gray question of goal-tending. When a defensive player blocks a shot while the ball is on a downward route to the basket, that is goal-tending—and I automatically award the basket to the shooter. But when a defensive player stops a ball on its way up, that's a legal block and play continues without interruption. In tonight's game Elmore Smith blocked at least ten Cleveland shots legally, but he was also called for goal-tending on four other occasions. Smith's predecessor, Wilt Chamberlain, also used to average about two legal blocks per goal-tending in every game.

The Powers Theory of Shot Blocking and Goal-tending is that goal-tending is impossible on any shot taken inside fifteen feet against a defensive player positioned halfway between the basket and the shooter. In other words, according to this theory, a player cannot shoot a fifteen-foot shot and have the ball on a downward flight in less than eight feet. Remember, if the defensive player stands more than eight feet away from the shooter, he is playing an illegal defense. So, under normal circumstances, it's a blocked shot—not goal-tending—when the Jabbars and the Cowenses and the Smiths and the Thurmonds of the NBA block those soft jumpers from about fifteen feet away from the basket. Okay, Euclid?

Wednesday, December 12 (off-day)

On the flight home from Cleveland it suddenly hit me that this has been the Year of the Injury in the NBA. Willis Reed, Earl Monroe and Wes Unseld all have had recurrences of their knee problems. Jerry West has had everything from pneumonia to a bad stomach to a bad leg. Jerry Sloan wears more bandages than a mummy. Cazzie Russell, Nate Thurmond and Clyde Lee all have spent more time on Golden State's disabled roster than the playing roster. Blue Cross will be raising its rates at the end of the year.

After the game in Cleveland I talked briefly with Happy Hairston of the Lakers, and Happy looked as happy as someone who had just been informed that his wife totaled his new Mercedes. "I'm not feeling well at all," Happy said sadly. "I need about a week's rest." Who doesn't? Listening to Hairston's problems reminded me of the ritual that Bill Russell and I always conducted before every Boston game I worked when Russell was still playing for the Celtics.

Russell was a champion hypochondriac. He always used the appearance of the officials for a game as his personal reminder that it was time to stop warming up and return to the bench and get ready for the game. So he'd take a last shot, turn and head for the Boston bench—all the while limping, coughing, shaking his hand, craning his neck, or twisting his back.

"Hi, Rich," he'd say to me.

"Hi, Bill," I'd answer. "How do you feel?"

"Terrible."

"Yeah," I'd say. "You do look a little pale."

"Yeah, man, that's how bad it is," Russell would say. Then he'd laugh that high-pitched cackle of his that could crack a wine glass at ten miles.

For a time I had another type of pre-game routine with Clyde Lovellette, the big center who played for St. Louis, Boston and a bunch of other clubs during his NBA career. "Wide" Clyde was a fast-draw expert and a real fan of Western movies. When I walked onto the court for a game, we would have a dueling contest patterned along the introductory scene to Gunsmoke.

Clyde did a fast Matt Dillon number, grabbing at his hip, pointing his forefinger in my direction, and then blowing imaginary smoke from his "gun muzzle" with a look of satisfaction. I'd put my "gun" to my heart and pretend I was falling to the floor. One time a reporter for a New York paper watched our shoot-out in stunned amazement and wrote a column about it the next day. Unfortunately the NBA did not appreciate the humor and ordered me to stop it at once. When orders come down from Olympus, Ol' Double D always listens.

Saturday, December 15 (Boston at Phoenix)

I caught the morning nonstop flight from New York to Phoenix and was resting in my motel room, watching a football game, at 12:30 P.M. According to the rules, referees are supposed to be in town the night before a game if such scheduling is possible, but I usually bend that rule to the breaking point. I don't take chances, mind you. For example, I checked with the airlines half a dozen times yesterday about the flying conditions forecast for today. If there was even the slightest possibility that my flight from New York would have been delayed because of bad weather this morning, I would have flown here yesterday. So, barring complications, I've become a confirmed day-of-game traveler except on trips to the West Coast.

Oddly enough, the late Bill Smith, who was one of my frequent partners in the old days of the NBA, and I were fired one year on the grounds that we had violated the rules and were not in Cincinnati early enough for a playoff game between the Celtics and the Royals. Bill actually had arrived the night before, and I checked in from New York at 9:00 A.M. the morning of the game, but Sid Borgia couldn't locate us all day and figured we hadn't landed until an hour or so before the game. So he marched into our dressing room before the game and summarily fired us. We worked that night, but did not work the next week of playoffs. Finally Borgia rescinded the dismissals after we presented fresh evidence that proved we both were in town at least eleven hours before the game. Still, it was a costly experience because in those days the officials were paid only for the playoff games they actually worked. The firing, in fact, cost me more than $1,000.

The Boston-Phoenix game tonight presented only one minor complication, which was a pleasant change following weeks of disputes, altercations and protests. On one play Neal Walk of the Suns accidentally ran over me as the ball rolled out of bounds. I got off the floor and gave the ball to Phoenix, a decision that prompted a major protest by the Celtics. Then young Bill Jones, my partner, came over and said that I should give the ball to Boston because it had gone out of bounds off a Phoenix player. So I did. You can't be KO'd and expect to make the correct call all the time.

The Celtics ran—repeat ran—to a 20-plus point lead at the half, but Charlie Scott rallied the Suns with 31 points in the second half and they closed to within 1 point with 12 seconds to play. However, Scott missed the go-ahead jump shot, and when Jo Jo White picked off the rebound, the Celtics appeared to have clinched the victory. But for some weird reason White tried to lob a pass to John Havlicek instead of simply controlling the ball and killing the clock with his dribbling. He overthrew Havlicek badly. Dick Van Arsdale took the errant pass and whipped it down court to Scott for an uncontested layup that gave the Suns a 121 to 120 lead. There were still four seconds left, though, and the Celtics managed to get off two good scoring chances—a baseline jumper by Havlicek and a tip-in attempt by Don Nelson. But both shots rolled off the rim—and Phoenix had scored an amazing come-from-behind victory.

Sunday, December 16 (Milwaukee at Portland)

Back to the old meatgrinder. We may have had a peaceful exhibition last night in Phoenix, but the Milwaukee-Portland battle royal tonight contained enough brawling and fighting to start a new series of Friday night fights.

It all started when Bob Dandridge of the Bucks and Sidney Wicks of the Trail Blazers were nose-to-nose on a pick play at the foul line, as Dandridge tried to block out Wicks so one of the Bucks could have an unimpeded shot at the basket. Then Dandridge pushed Wicks away. Bill Jones and I both saw Dandridge's foul perfectly, and we both blew our whistles. Jones, however, was closer to the action so he handled the call. As Jones was signaling to the scorer's table, Wicks suddenly pushed Dandridge. Then the barrage of dirty verbiage began. Moments later Wicks put up his dukes, John L. Sullivan style, and Dandridge did the same. Wicks threw the first punch and connected solidly. Seeing this, I moved toward the combatants to play peacemaker. When I stepped between them Dandridge went around me in an attempt to get back at Wicks, and he

pushed me away like a fly. Oscar Robertson tried to inter-
vene, but he had no success in quelling the fight. Now
Wicks was moving backward, egging Dandridge on. All the
other players on the court were spectators.

As the fight continued, Dandridge hit Wicks with a shot,
then both players collided and tackled one another. By the
time the melee ended, Dandridge and Wicks were two rows
deep into the seats at center court. We finally separated
them, and I promptly ejected both of them from the game.

Wicks left the floor with a cut hand. Dandridge retired
with a loose tooth. Moments later the public address announcer switched on his microphone and said: "Would the
doctor please report to the Milwaukee dressing room!"
The remark tickled the Portland fans. What inane thinking!
Nobody won the fight. Both players lost. The fans lost.
And, most important, basketball lost.

Harry Glickman, general manager of the Portland team,
came into our dressing rooms after the battle and asked me
why I had ejected Wicks. My comments were precise. "If
Dandridge had not attacked Wicks after Wicks had thrown
the first punch, it would have been just a punching foul on
Wicks. However, when Dandridge responded to Wicks'
punch with a punch of his own, they both were guilty of
fighting—and out they went." Glickman claimed he had not
seen Wicks throw the first punch. Then he peppered me
with a dozen questions all prefaced with "What if."

I don't want any "what ifs" in my games. I only act on
"what *is*." Still, Bill Jones and I were the villains, so far as
the fans in Portland were concerned. The Trail Blazers lost
the game, so their fans blamed the officials. So what else is
new in the world?

Monday, December 17 (off-day)

The headline over the basketball story in the morning Portland paper read: "Fight-Marred Game." There

were several pictures accompanying Neil Anderson's story, but the caption writer called the fisticuffs only a "slight scuffle." The headline writer and the caption writer ought to get their heads together. Mr. Anderson was highly critical of my role in the altercation, suggesting I should not have ejected Wicks because Dandridge started the incident. To illustrate his point, he referred to a television game I had refereed last year when Kareem Abdul-Jabbar KO'd Happy Hairston. Jabbar not only was not ejected, he did not even get a foul—or so Mr. Anderson reported.

Not true. It was the game in which the Bucks broke the Lakers record winning streak at thirty-three by trouncing them in Milwaukee. What happened was that Jabbar attempted a stuff shot and Hairston came at him with a body block. I was under the basket and called a foul on Hairston. Both players hit the floor hard, with Jabbar falling heavily on his knees. Jabbar's first reaction to the tackle was to throw a punch at Hairston, a looping right hand that barely nicked Hairston. Listen, I saw the punch. It was hardly a fight.

As Jabbar moved to his left, I leaped in, in an attempt to stop him and prevent others from getting involved. Enter Wilt Chamberlain. Suddenly I was standing between an angry Jabbar and a menacing Chamberlain, which must have been quite a sight. I put my hands up and stopped Chamberlain's advance. Then I called personal fouls on both Hairston and Jabbar. End of incident.

The league office called me the next morning and asked why I had not ejected Jabbar. I told Johnny Nucatola that if Jabbar's punch had landed solidly, I would have ejected him. But it was a grazing punch at best. And very ineffectual. Also, it was one punch, not a series of blows, and it was done in a fit of pique. In no way was Jabbar's action premeditated. So Jabbar took his foul shot, Hairston took his—and Los Angeles got the ball at mid-court. The game was well under control.

The main thrust of Mr. Anderson's story was that referees protect superstars of the magnitude of a Jabbar but could care less what happens to the other players in a game. I take umbrage with Mr. Anderson's comments. He has the ears and the eyes of the sporting public here, and today he deprecated not only Richie Powers but all the referees in the NBA. He indicted us. So, for the second time in my life, I have written a letter to a newspaper, and not only to Mr. Anderson but also to his sports editor. Then I called New York and told Johnny Nucatola what I had done. In the letter I told Mr. Anderson that he was wrong in his assumptions, that if he had been more professional in his job he would have come into our dressing room after the game and asked me about the Dandridge-Wicks episode. I asked him not for a retraction but for a statement of pure fact. I don't need his opinion. I know what happened. He doesn't. (By the way, I never heard back from Mr. Anderson.)

It's a nebulous point, really. The rule book says that referees can eject a player when they judge the player's actions to be flagrant. Jabbar's actions were not flagrant. Personally, I'd love to assess a technical foul every time I see a player fire an elbow that misses. In all these situations, it comes down to a question of the referee's judgment. If a man throws a punch and misses, I can call it a punching foul. If he throws an elbow and misses, though, I can't call anything. It's right there in the book. Maybe they ought to change the rules.

Tuesday, December 18 (Boston at Golden State)

The Golden State Warriors made a fatal mistake tonight: they tried to run with the Celtics for 48 minutes. They managed to succeed for 24 minutes and trailed by only 2 points as the big crowd in Oakland cheered them on. In the second half, though, the Celtics switched into over-drive—and roared away to an easy win. Cazzie Russell is still hurt. Nate Thurmond wore himself to a frazzle trying to keep up with Dave Cowens. And Rick Barry ran so much that his legs were rubbery and wobbly at the end.

At halftime I called the airport and checked on my post-game flight to Detroit. The reservations girl informed me there was a blizzard in the Great Lakes area and that she was making no promises about getting me to Detroit. Great. I called Johnny Nucatola in New York and advised him of the situation. He told me not to worry. He'll call Lenny Wirtz in Buffalo and have him standby there for instructions.

Wednesday, December 19 (Chicago at Detroit)

Like the mail, the referees always get through. I landed in a blizzard at 7:30 A.M. and called Nucatola to advise him that I had made it to Detroit. To the airport, that is. It took me another three hours to negotiate the trip downtown to the hotel. As I walked into my hotel room, the phone was ringing. It was Ed Batogowski, my game partner, calling from Grand Rapids. His plane from New York had been rerouted there because of the snowstorm. Ed said he would make the game if he had to take a dogsled across the state. Sure enough, he reached the hotel about an hour before game time after a harrowing trip in a rental car. "If I never see snow again, it will be too soon," he said grumpily.

Predictably, the Detroit-Chicago game was another bruiser. Detroit and Chicago *always* play bruising basketball games. Early in the first quarter—in fact, after less than 20 seconds of play—Bob Love of the Bulls grabbed his thigh and asked for a 20-second injury time out. He told me that one of the Pistons had grabbed him on the thigh, injuring him. I hadn't seen the incident, but I gave him the brief respite anyway. Moments later, as play resumed, Chet Walker of the Bulls drove the baseline against Willie Norwood, and Norwood stepped into his path and knocked him down into a heap. After whistling the foul, I moved to get the loose basketball. Suddenly Walker vaulted through the air and attempted to throw a punch at the unsuspecting Norwood. Fortunately for everyone involved, Batogowski was right on the spot and stepped between the two combatants.

Right then something struck me. These things don't just happen. Oh, they happen, but not with that much violence, that much fury, that much combativeness so early in a game. Then I remembered watching a recent Pistons-Bulls game on television. There were a number of altercations in that game, too. And now the problem was live, staring me in the face. So I called the two captains—Walker of the Bulls and Dave Bing of the Pistons—to the center of the court and warned them that any player who made a fist and attempted to throw a punch would be summarily ejected from the game. Seconds later Bob Lanier of the Pistons picked off a rebound and was fouled by Jerry Sloan of the Bulls. As we started back up the court, Lanier and Sloan engaged in a loud shouting match. I made a speech to both of them, particularly to Lanier, who uses some strong language at times.

Really, though, there is nothing a referee can do once players begin to excoriate one another. I can stop a fight —but not a shouting contest. Still, I think that verbal wars go beyond the realm of sportsmanship, so I told Lanier and Sloan to cease and desist immediately. I said to Lanier, "If you pursue that type of language"—and didn't have to say anything else. He got the message, and he apologized.

Awhile later Dick Motta, the Chicago coach, started a verbal attack on Batogowski during a time out. I interrupted him and said: "Listen, Dick, I'm not fooling around tonight." Ooops! The moment I said it, I worried that Motta might think that, hell, Powers had been fooling around in the other games. What I meant was that I was not abiding by any of Motta's verbiage tonight. He got the message.

Everything settled down. In fact, neither team took a free throw in the second quarter. Detroit won by 2 points in what turned out to be a great game because, I think, Ed and I made them play basketball—not football. We kept the game within the 92-by-50 boundaries.

Thursday, December 20 (Off-Day)

Batogowski and I spent four hours waiting at the Detroit airport for our post-game flight to New York and did not land at Newark until 3:00 A.M. Ed dropped me in Greenwich shortly before 5:00 A.M. and then continued on to his home in Southington, Connecticut. I woke up at 1:00 P.M. and called Ed to thank him for the ride home, but he wasn't there. His wife said he arrived home at 6:15 A.M., napped for ninety minutes and then left for school at 7:45 A.M. Ed is a physical-education instructor at a high school near Hartford. God, you've got to admire the man's dedication.

Friday, December 21 (Off-Day)

I have watched so many basketball games on television this season that I began to wonder how I function on the court myself. So I took the train into New York today and spent several hours watching films of three games I have worked in recent weeks. Unfortunately, the films were two dimensional and did not show any on-court depth. I saw a lot of fouls committed on those films, but I did not know whether I had called them or not. Maybe I did. Maybe I didn't. Maybe my partner did. Maybe he didn't. It was all very confusing. The films are for player consumption, not the referees; we are left on the cutting room floor.

Johnny Nucatola watched the movies with me, and he

said that one coach had questioned a call I had made in one game. The winning coach, mind you. That's how finite this game is getting. I probably blow my whistle two hundred times in a game, and the winning coach, of all people, is complaining that I may have made a bad call. *A* bad call. Not two or three or ten or fifty or two hundred. Ridiculous! Johnny and I discussed the complaint, but I couldn't remember the play. The coach said it was right there on the film, but we didn't see it. We played it back a dozen times —but never saw the foul he so stubbornly insisted was there. Cripes, we're vulnerable to every loose comment, every adverse remark muttered by all the coaches and all the players. Thank God we can stand up to these pressures.

Anyway, I'm not going to watch any more films. Period.

Saturday, December 22 (Cleveland at Atlanta)

Cleveland upset Atlanta in an uneventful game at the Omni. On the way to his dressing room Hawks Coach Cotton Fitzsimmons said that the Cavaliers victory was an early Christmas present from the Atlanta players. What was it that the football people used to say: "On any given Sunday any given team in the NFL can upset any other team in the NFL." Well, on any given Saturday any given team in the NBA can upset any other team in the NBA.

Sunday, December 23 (Capital *vs.* Buffalo at Toronto)

The trouble with working night games in Toronto is that there are never any late-night flights back to New York. So after the Buffalo Braves beat the Bullets tonight, Mark Mano and I had to wind-down around the hotel and place a wake-up call for 5:45 A.M. tomorrow in order to catch the first flight back home.

Tuesday, December 25 (off-day)

There are two games scheduled today in the NBA. Merry Christmas!

Wednesday, December 26 (K.C.–Omaha at Houston)

Mark Mano and I were partners again tonight—the third straight game we have worked as a team. The league, I think, would like to establish about six set teams of officials and have them work together at all times. It's not as easy as it sounds. Officials must be in tune psychologically as well as physically. They must maintain a rapport and be willing to call on their partners for assistance when they need it. They must put aside their off-court feelings, regardless of what they are. And what happens when a team of officials is broken up? What happens when a young referee goes from, say, a Richie Powers to a Mendy Rudolph? Or from a Powers to a younger official? Psychologically, it's a problem.

The tendency seems to be that senior officials are asked to take control of the toughest situations, and I, for one, don't like it. I want younger officials to become more assertive. On the court they have the same power as the older official. They should not have any trepidation about making a call or adhering to the rules. Too many young officials have this foible. They don't think they have the right to get angry and assertive during a game. Why not? It's their job —and their life. If a player presses them, they must remain firm and press back. The rules are on the side of the referee. If he enforces them, he won't have any problems.

Two men can do this job beautifully if both strive to do it equally. One man can—and should—compensate for his partner's inadequacies, whatever they may be. You must know your partner almost as well as you know yourself. Areas he does not function well in, you must function beautifully in. And the word "idiosyncracy" comes into my mind. We all have idiosyncracies—and we must compensate for them.

Young referees have come up to me over the years and said: "I had a bad game." Hogwash. You can't have a bad game. I know I've never had a bad game myself. If a referee has a bad night once every eighty games, then he's a rotten official. Baseball players hit .300—and they are superstars. Basketball players shoot 50 percent—and they are heroes. Hockey players score on 12 percent of their shots—and they make the all-star team. Great. But referees can't be that way. We must be 100 percent at all times. Teams will not tolerate officials who are right only 99 percent of the time. And the league office certainly won't tolerate them either.

Lo the poor referee who doesn't realize what his lot happens to be! There's no penultimate in this job. Only the ultimate. Do your job—or be dismissed. The loneliness and the pressure get to me, but the way I combat the problem is to immerse myself deeper into the business at hand. Referees can never take a casual attitude to their job.

I'm a martinet, I guess. Every player in the NBA knows who Richie Powers is. Every coach in the NBA knows who Richie Powers is. And I'm sure that a lot of NBA fans know who Richie Powers is. I have established myself over the years. Moreover, the players and coaches know where I draw the fine line. Well, this is what our young officials must do, too.

Friday, December 28 (Atlanta at Chicago)

Speaking of young officials, I worked with Tommy Nunez for the first time tonight—and he was very impressive. Give us a couple more young referees with Tommy's personality and temperament and we'll never have any officiating problems. Tommy told me he wants to make refereeing his career. I told him—jokingly, of course—that he was nuts. Unfortunately, we didn't have a chance to spend much time together because I flew home immediately after the game, but I hope we work one of those three-games-in-three-nights tours in the near future.

The Atlanta-Chicago game was ultra-physical, Chicago style. Shortly after the opening tap-off Bob Love of the Bulls put his elbow under Lou Hudson's chin and kept it there. Hudson was understandably irate and said to Love, "Don't throw any elbows at me," and threw a punch. Love retaliated, but their blows were errant. Love, who stands about 6 feet 8 inches, and Hudson, who goes about 6 feet 5 inches, were finally separated. What the hell goes on in this league?

Then, for about the hundredth time in the last two weeks, I repeated my speech about closed fists and ejections. When I finished, I looked at Chet Walker, who had played peacemaker, and said: "Hey, didn't I say all this to you people recently?"

The game quieted down for a while, but in the third quarter Love went up for a jump shot in such a way that the defensive player was very close to him, practically chest-to-chest. In releasing the ball, Love hit the defensive player's arms—and the ball missed the basket by a wide margin. "Call the ——foul!" Love yelled. I did. I called a technical foul on Love for saying the magic word and ejected him from the game. At the next whistle Walker walked over. "Bob didn't curse at you," he said. I almost laughed. "Love told me to call the ——foul," I said to Walker. "Everybody in the building heard him, and I am not abiding by that language." Walker nodded and walked away.

Howard Porter replaced Love, and midway through the final period he landed on his back during some rebounding action under the basket. The Bulls asked for a 20-second injury time out, which I gave them. But when Porter was still on the floor after the 20 seconds had elapsed I told Dick Motta that he had to call a regular time out. Motta

(84)

mentioned something about getting a stretcher for Porter.
I sympathized with him but said he still had to call the time
out.

Motta said: "Richie, you've lost your sense of humor."

"What?" I said.

"You've lost your sense of humor," Motta repeated.

"Well, say something funny."

"Okay. I think I'm talking to God," Motta said.

"Oh, yeah? What team does He play for?" I said.

Was that funny? Anyway, Motta called the time out—and
that's all I really cared about.

Sunday, December 30 (Detroit at Milwaukee)

Detroit closed out the year by blitzing the Bucks in
Milwaukee as Dave Bing gave a spectacular exhibition of
perimeter shooting, connecting on just about every shot he
threw at the basket. Late in the first quarter, after several
successive Bing baskets, the Bucks called a time out and Jon
McGlocklin, who was covering Bing, turned around and
threw the ball disgustedly into the stands. I thought maybe
he was tossing it to his brother or his wife or some friend
—anything to get it away from Bing. Still, I had no re-
course. I had to call a technical for delay of game.

At halftime one of the broadcasters asked me why I called
a delay of game technical when time already was out. Listen. It's a matter of semantics. There is no way I can allow
a player to fire the ball into the stands at any time, otherwise it would happen all the time—and we would run out
of basketballs. Oddly, technicals for delay of game do not
count toward the rule that stipulates that two technicals
automatically mean ejection, so when McGlocklin received
another technical foul later in the game he still was allowed
to remain on the floor. Only unsportsmanlike-conduct
technicals count toward ejection. On his second technical,
McGlocklin was dribbling up court almost in isolation, with

no Piston in sight. On all courts there are some places that are harder than others, particularly at the joists, and sometimes the ball will bounce very high off these points. Well, the ball bounced high into the air while McGlocklin was dribbling, and he palmed it, thus causing a turnover. McGlocklin reacted with a stream of verbiage and a lot of arm waving, so I reacted by giving him the technical.

On the way to the dressing room after the game, Bob Rakel and I were confronted by a fifteen-year-old monster with an incredibly dirty mouth. He called us every name in the book, and some that weren't in any book. Tell me. What kind of upbringing can a kid like that have? If he were my kid, he'd get a mouthful of soap and a good paddling.

It was zero outside—and seemed even colder in the dressing room. We had planned to take our time getting dressed, since there was no place to go on a Sunday night in Milwaukee, but the arctic conditions changed our minds. I ran for the showers, but they didn't work. The showers in the Bucks dressing room worked, and the showers in the Pistons dressing room worked, but the showers in the referees' room didn't. Figure that out. Maybe someone came into our room and disconnected the valves. Maybe the building superintendant was so depressed by Milwaukee's loss that he turned off the pressure. Maybe I'm getting paranoid.

Tuesday, January 1 (Chicago at Golden State)

I spent a quiet evening in Greenwich, ushering in the New Year with several Double Ds, and then was up at 6:00 A.M. to catch the first flight from New York to San Francisco. That's cutting it a little fine, but no way was I going to spend New Year's Eve alone in a motel room. Like most referees, I didn't have much time to enjoy the holidays. And now I'll be on the West Coast for most of the next week.

Before the Golden State–Chicago game I wished all the

Hugh Evans and Ol'
Number 26 walk into
the Milwaukee Arena
for the start of a
long night's work.

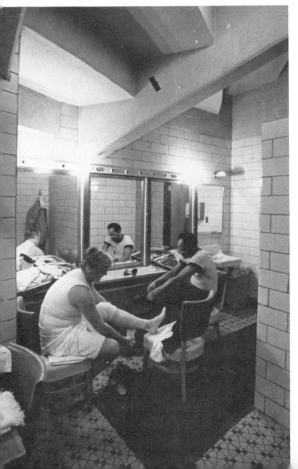

Before each game
I tape my left leg from
ankle to thigh to prevent
recurrences of pulled
muscle injuries.

*Photographs by
Heinz Kluetmeier*

Jim McMillian of the Buffalo Braves and I enjoy some pre-game banter. It's pre-game because we are smiling—not finger waving.

I always mark the game ball with a ball-point pen so one—and only one—ball will be used throughout the game. No "switchies" at halftime.

One, two . . . touch your toes. Yes, Double D can still touch his toes.

My last moment
of peace.

Game Time.
Jabbar jumps with
McAdoo — and the show
goes on.

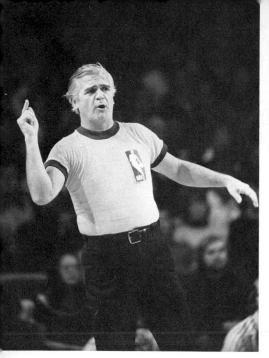

It's an offensive foul.

A push-off with the left arm.

Maestro Powers Conducting

Geez, what a collision!
Will he ever get up?

He *is* getting up.

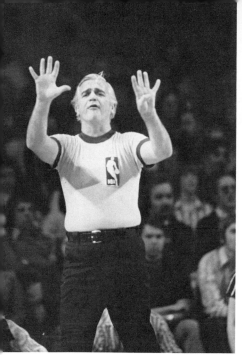

The foul is on Number 54.

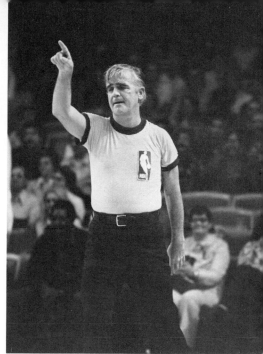

We're going that way now.

Foul on Number 25! (Judging from
my pained expression, perhaps he
deserves twelve shots.)

Two minutes later:
"Baby, you just walked!"

No foul here, that's obvious. I am in a perfect position to see the necessary gap between shooter and defender as Bob McAdoo pops a fadeaway jumper over Kareem Abdul-Jabbar.

Finding reverse gear. Buffalo has just scored and Milwaukee races up court. The Braves intercept and Powers does an abrupt about face. I dash between Jabbar and McAdoo, leap out of Kareem's way so he can move against his Buffalo opponent, and make a one-point landing as McAdoo sets up for his shot. Two points for the Braves.

Back to the dressing room after the game. Believe it or not, the little fellow at the right actually asked me for my autograph.

Nice game, Hugh!

It's all over — for another twenty-four hours.

starting players a Happy New Year, and Bob Love of the Bulls responded by solemnly saying he had made a New Year's resolution "not to talk to the officials." Love was referring to the incident of the magic word in Chicago last week. "Bob, those things happen," I said. "There's nothing to worry about, unless you say it again." After Love walked away, center Dennis Awtrey of the Bulls leaned over and asked: "Richie, what *is* that word we can't say?"

The Bulls ripped the Warriors, holding them to just 25 points in the first half and at one point galloping to a 39-point lead. Rick Barry had a strange game. Normally Rick will shoot the ball from anyplace on the court. Uptown. Downtown. The pivot. Every place. In this game he hardly shot at all. Instead, he tried to be the playmaker. Why? I don't know. Sometimes Rick receives criticism for all the shots he takes; perhaps he was going the other way just to shut up the critics. He was open for some good shots on numerous occasions but instead chose to pass the ball to a teammate. As a result, the Warriors probably set a world indoor record for 3-second violations. When Barry has the ball, he normally shoots it—so the other Warriors, anticipating the shot, move into rebounding positions under the basket. In tonight's game Barry wasn't shooting, and all those rebounders were trapped under the basket for more than the legal 3 seconds. The Warriors were a very confused club tonight.

Wednesday, January 2 (Buffalo at Seattle)

Referees are not supposed to fraternize with the players or the coaches at any time, but occasionally it is hard for us to avoid them. This morning, for instance, I was flying from Oakland to Seattle and the Chicago team happened to be on the same flight. We all exchanged pleasantries while boarding the plane, and then we went our separate ways. Midway through the flight, however, Chet

(87)

Walker stopped by my seat and asked me if I had read the article in *Sport Magazine* where Mendy Rudolph and Johnny Nucatola discussed the three-referee system now used by some college basketball conferences. I told Chet I had not read the story, but I explained my feelings on the subject to him.

Nucatola first tried to sell the three-referee concept to the colleges about twenty years ago. However, plainly and simply, it is financially extravagant, particularly now when colleges—and, for that matter, the pro leagues—are trying to cut down their costs. Sure, one more pair of eyes would help control a game. Nevertheless, as I told Chet, I think it's much easier for me to control a game when I am in visual and mental contact with my partner—and there is no way any official can expect to establish such a rapport with two other referees.

For example, on a charging foul or an out-of-bounds play, it is pretty easy for two minds to meet and make a decision because one man can convince the other that he saw something first—or better. With three officials, we'd have a third pair of eyes, a third brain and a third opinion —and we'd be in a quandry. I can control my partner, and he can control me—but what about that third referee? Listen. We don't need three men on the court to govern the actions of ten men.

My final point was that I thought it was tough enough these days to get good referees and that it would be totally impossible to develop strong officials under the three-man system. Referees develop themselves by being thrown into the pit. If referees learn by sitting, studying, watching and acting as the third man, we might end up with a picture referee who has a headful of eggshells.

Chet also asked me if referees hold grudges against players who have given them trouble. I told him that any referee who holds a grudge should not be allowed to work in the league. I explained that our problem is to maintain control of the game under the rules and specifications laid down by the league office. We don't make the rules, the league office and the rules committee establish the law. We follow them —and enforce them. I told him that I never look for a foul to call on a player because of some past difficulties with the individual. The day I do that will be the day I retire.

Of course, there are personality clashes between some officials and some players and coaches. I imagine there are officials who dislike certain players, and I suspect there are players and coaches who dislike certain officials. It's a mutual admiration society. However, I have never carried, and will never carry, a grudge against any player. Nowadays the NBA is so big that we never really get to know the players personally, which I think is a mistake. According to the rules, Walker and I were not supposed to engage in this conversation. But we did—and we are both better off for it. I, for one, think there should be a greater rapport among coaches, players and officials. Communication might make things more understandable all the way around.

I asked Walker if the NBA's players' association was conducting an evaluation of the referees. Earlier in the year Dave DeBusschere of the Knicks was ejected from a game; the next day a reporter saw Dave writing away during a plane trip. When asked what he was doing, DeBusschere said he was evaluating the referees. Walker admitted that such a study was presently underway. I asked him if the players were doing it constructively. He said that he hoped they were. Great! If the study is done that way, without regard for personal feeling, it can help all the officials. If the players come to an agreement on what they think Powers should do better on the court, and come up with concrete suggestions, then I'm all for it. But if they simply come to an agreement that "Powers stinks,"—well, that's hardly helpful.

Most of the Bulls took a busman's holiday and came out to the Buffalo-Seattle game, and I'm sure they all wondered what the officials and coaches were laughing about during the pre-game meeting at center court. According to NBA rules, coaches must wear a shirt and tie during the game. Bill Russell rarely wears a shirt and tie, but he was wearing one tonight, while Jack Ramsay, the Buffalo coach, was outfitted with a turtleneck sweater. "That's a ten-dollar fine," I said to Ramsay. Russell's roaring laugh could have been heard in Tacoma.

Ramsay was laughing at the end, though, when Ernie DiGregorio hit on several long shots and won the game for Buffalo. The score was tied eight times during the last five minutes, and both clubs combined to hit nine straight shots down the stretch. Ernie D is an amazing rookie, and he no doubt will be an easy winner of the rookie-of-the-year award. Cue-Ball Watts, the bald rookie guard of the Super-Sonics, was all over Ernie D at the end, but he still couldn't stop him. For a change I didn't call any technical fouls either, and there were no fights in the game. Maybe the players are mellowing.

Friday, January 4 (Houston at Portland)

My partner on this West Coast junket is Mark Schlafman, who is the idol of all the officials in the NBA because he resides in Miami, Florida. I was telling him about all the snow we had around New York during the holiday season, and he didn't express any sympathy except to report that the average temperature in Miami in December was 81 degrees.

Sitting in our dressing room before the Houston-Portland game, I told Mark we probably would have difficulty trying to maintain control of the action because of the Houston team's debating tactics. The Rockets ought to change their names to the Filibusters. When one team debates the referees all night, the opposition begins to debate the officials, too. So Houston games became meetings of the forensic society.

Sure enough, Jack Marin of the Rockets promptly got on

me from the bench. Finally I walked over to Marin and warned him that I had heard enough. Twenty seconds later Marin entered the game, and forty seconds later he exited the game via an ejection. I don't think he ever handled the ball while he was on the floor. What happened was that one of the Portland players drove around Marin and went up for an easy shot, only to be fouled by Marin in the act of shooting. When I called the foul, Marin leaped into the air, screamed "Jesus Christ!" and then did a dance around the floor. *Tweet!* Seeing my signal, Marin jumped into the air again and yelled "Jesus —— Christ!" *Tweet!!*

"You'll never get the money!" Marin shouted as he stormed off the floor. I don't know why the players think the referees collect the $50 fine for every technical foul they call. The league collects the money, not me.

Later in the game I had another debate with the Rockets, this one involving Egan and center Don Smith about another rim-hanging episode. Smith slam-dunked the ball and then hung on the rim in order to protect a player under him from getting stepped on, but according to the rules I had to give him a technical for it. However, I will call the league office tomorrow and explain the Smith technical to Johnny Nucatola, and I doubt that Smith will be assessed the $50 fine. Egan was incensed at the technical and said, "Richie, are you deliberately trying my patience tonight? Are you deliberately seeing how far I'll let you go?" I took a deep breath. "You can go with Marin if you continue this discussion any longer!" A rule is a rule is a rule.

Despite all the time and effort the Houston players wasted during their debates, they still had enough energy left to beat the Trail Blazers. Calvin Murphy got hot at the end and hit from everywhere on the court. The Trail Blazers played their usual unpredictable game. At the start they did a lot of driving toward the basket, with Sidney Wicks and Geoff Petrie scoring consistently from close in. Then, for some inexplicable reason, they changed their game plan and threw up a lot of poor shots from the perimeter.

Sunday, January 6 (K.C.–Omaha at Los Angeles)

The trouble with this trip is all the off days between games. We had an off day on Thursday in Portland, and we had an off day yesterday here. When I'm on the road I want to be working, not sitting around a hotel room for two days and waiting for a game. It can get pretty boring. The Lakers-Kings game was mild compared to the problems we had up in Portland. Nate Archibald was back in the K.C.–Omaha line-up after recovering from his achilles-tendon injury, and he spent most of the game bouncing off the Lakers on his forays to the basket.

To some observers, Archibald spends the night getting fouled, but he creates many of the situations himself by caroming off bigger players on his serpentine thrusts down the lane. He probably fouls as much as he gets fouled. Even with Archibald in the Kings line-up, and Jerry West still missing from the Los Angeles line-up, the Lakers were too strong for the visitors and pulled away to a comfortable win.

My only problem in the game was a questionable decision on an out-of-bounds play. I remember talking with Johnny Kundla, then the coach of the Minneapolis Lakers, and Jim Pollard, one of Kundla's star players, during my rookie season as a referee and asking them what they thought was the toughest call an official had to make. They both claimed it was the out-of-bounds play when several players were battling for possession of the ball. Over the years the out-of-bounds call has been just that: the toughest decision I have ever had to make.

Midway through the Lakers-Kings game it appeared to me that Nate Williams of the Kings had deflected the ball out of bounds with his leg. As such, it was a kicking violation—and Los Angeles' ball. When I signaled the kicking infraction, Williams claimed ball hadn't touched him. I turned and asked Schlafman if I had missed the call, but he said that he hadn't seen the play through the maze of

(92)

bodies in front of him. So I was prepared to give the ball to Los Angeles until Williams' pleading type of argument —a sort of, "Richie, how could you make such a mistake?" —convinced me that I had indeed made a mistake. I gave the ball to the Kings, and the Lakers—to their credit— didn't offer any argument. They realized I had made a mistake in the first place. Referees can—and should— change their calls when their error is obvious.

Wednesday, January 9 (Cleveland at Philadelphia)

The snow was blowing so hard in the northeast corridor that I had to take the train from New York to Philadelphia. Poor Mark Schlafman. He spent Monday and Tuesday in sunny Miami, and now he's walking around in two feet of snow. I told him I could get him a good deal on a used overcoat.

Philadelphia is my jinx town because nothing ever seems to go right for me here. Some July they'll ask me to come down and referee a charity game or something, and the game will be postponed because of a blizzard—or maybe the train from New York will hit a cow.

Early in the game I was running down court and accidentally crashed into a cement wall named Austin Carr of the Cleveland Cavaliers. I flew one way, arms and legs in a tangle, and my whistle flew the other. My knees hit my jaw in the collision, and later, when they handed me my whistle, I found I couldn't close my mouth. Of course, some players and coaches will agree that I have never been able to keep my mouth shut. The Philadelphia trainer worked on the jaw and finally managed to get it back into whistling order. But, God, was I ever sore. Maybe I should wear shoulder pads.

My injury was minor, though, compared to what happened to Lenny Wilkens of the Cavaliers. Lenny was driving down the lane, and I was the official under the basket. As Lenny jumped into the air, Leroy Ellis—a fellow St.

(93)

John's man, by the way—jumped up to block his shot. But Wilkens anticipated Leroy's block, so he stopped in midair and tried to pass the ball to a trailing teammate. Seeing this, Leroy threw out his left hand and made slight contact with Wilkens. Foul or no foul? Wilkens was not shooting the ball, contact seemed slight—so I waved off the play and let the action continue. Well, as it turned out, Ellis made more than slight contact with Wilkens—he broke Lenny's nose on the play.

There was no great controversy over my decision not to call a foul. Lenny and I even laughed about the incident later, if you can laugh with a fractured nose. All this proved a point to me: call what you see. Some people think referees live with the motto: "No harm, No foul." We don't—or at least I don't. In this case I should have called what I had seen.

Friday January 11 (Los Angeles at Boston)

More treacherous weather. I took the limousine from Greenwich to LaGuardia in order to catch a shuttle flight to Boston, but LaGuardia was closed down and Boston was socked in, too, so I rented a car and drove to Boston instead. Mark Schlafman was waiting for me when I arrived in the dressing room, and he didn't look like the happiest man in America. Then again, why should a Floridian be happy in a snowstorm?

The Lakers muffled the Celtics fast break and beat them handily. Midway through the game I had the privilege and honor of giving the ball to John Havlicek after he scored the 20,000th point of his distinguished NBA career. The capacity crowd in the Boston Garden cheered John loud and long, and the applause continued as the game resumed and Gail Goodrich of the Lakers was waiting to take a couple of free throws.

"Does the noise bother you?" I asked Goodrich. "If it

does, we can wait for it to subside before you have to shoot."

Goodrich said he couldn't hear the noise, yet I could hardly hear what he said because of the uproar. He took the free throws and made both of them. The man must be made of ice.

Saturday, January 12 (Milwaukee at Chicago)

On the flight from Boston to Chicago I bought *Sport Magazine* and read the story about the three-referee system. Who proofreads these stories anyway? One caption says that the player quoted above is a 5-foot 6-inch forward on one of the expansion teams. Hell, there aren't any 5-foot 6-inch forwards in the NBA that I know of. Anyway, this 5-foot 6-inch forward says that if referees are really serious about their jobs, they'd sit around their dressing room for half an hour before the game and discuss the teams playing that night.

Well, this 5-foot 6-inch forward on an expansion team is such a consummate ass that he doesn't know referees do sit in our dressing room for at least half an hour before every game and discuss the teams that will be playing on the court. And that's all we talk about. Tell me, where do people come up with all of this information that they throw around with such nonchalant expertise?

The article is really intriguing. The writer never quotes players by name, he just identifies them as, in one instance, a 6-foot 9-inch black guard with a two-hand set shot—or best known for his two-hand set shot. What black guard in the NBA has a two-hand set? What a laugh. And the writer talks about the special treatment referees give white players in relation to the treatment accorded to black players. Christ, that went out with McKinley. I believe the author didn't identify the player making that charge about preferential treatment because he knew he would have a libel suit on his hands. In another part of the story he mentions something about short, fat guards. The last short, fat guard in the NBA was Fat Freddy Scolari, and he retired about twenty years ago. I wonder if the writer has been to a basketball game in the last decade.

I think I'll stop reading newspapers and magazines before I get an ulcer.

And, if any sportswriters are in the audience, Manny Sokol and I spent about an hour tonight discussing the Bulls and the Bucks before the start of the game. Nothing serious, but our minds were riveted on the game. We didn't exchange jokes or swap stories or write letters or sign autographs or make phone calls. We worked.

The Bulls struggled to stay with the Bucks for a half, and they managed to remain within three points, 51 to 48, despite the absence of the injured Jerry Sloan. Without Sloan, the Bulls are not as aggressive as they normally are. He is their Havlicek, their Frazier, their Haywood, their Lanier and their Robertson. He is, you might say, their cohesive force. Then, taking advantage of Sloan's absence, the Bucks roared away to a big victory in the second half.

Sunday, January 13 (Philadelphia at Cleveland)

The one time I really wouldn't mind being in Houston, here I am in beautiful downtown Cleveland, Ohio, watching the Super Bowl game on television in my hotel room. If I had refereed the football game down in Houston, Larry Csonka wouldn't have run over the Minnesota Vikings with such reckless abandon because I'd have called a couple of thousand charging fouls on him.

The Cavaliers and Philadelphia are still struggling to find an identity. Except for Lenny Wilkens of the Cavaliers, there was no one player on either team capable of controlling the play in this game. When Wilkens did not have the ball, the game became a contest of hodge-podge, hodge-podge, who's got the ball? Both teams played the same way, although I can't describe what way that way was—and I don't think they can, either.

In the end Cleveland scraped out a 2-point win when I had to call something I can't ever remember calling in the closing seconds of a tight game. The Cavaliers led by 2 points, but the 76ers had the ball, and Freddy Carter was dribbling down the baseline when he suddenly turned, stopped, reversed direction, put his right foot down, hooked around the defender—and walked. No doubt about it, he walked. Freddy came over not to argue about the walk, but to insist he had been fouled. "I'm sorry," I said. "I never saw a foul." My partner, Bill Jones, obviously didn't see any foul either, because he didn't call it.

The remark by Carter put me in a quandary. Was he fouled and thus forced to walk? Hell, you can't think about those things after the call. You call what you see. And I received no argument from the Philadelphia bench after I made the call, not one single word. Gene Shue and Jack McMahon are teaching their young kids to play an honest game. They control their team, and they don't tolerate wild and uncontrolled incidents during moments of personal frustration. I wish more coaches were that way.

On the way to the dressing room after the game I asked Bill Fitch, the Cleveland coach, if he thought there was an inordinate amount of bitching being done by coaches this year. He said most definitely yes. He also said the bitching was deserved because, in his opinion, the standard of refereeing was down this year.

Then I asked him if he thought that technical fouls were becoming a joke among the players. He nodded. What does $50 mean to a guy who makes $150,000 a year? I suggested that perhaps for certain technical fouls we should be able to eject the guilty player for a certain period of time. Fitch thought it was an intriguing proposition, but he doubted that the NBA rules committee would ever adopt such a recommendation. My thinking on technicals, as I have stated repeatedly, is that the punitive value is considerably more important than the monetary value. Once players realize they will be lost to their team for a period of time after committing a technical, I'm sure that the frequency of technicals would decrease tremendously. And the game would be better for it.

Fitch told me he feels there is a definite lack of rapport between coaches and officials in the NBA. He blamed this problem on the rules, which state that coaches can only air their grievances to Johnny Nucatola and his chief aide, Mendy Rudolph. He said that he, for one, would much rather confront individual officials face to face in an attempt to work out the problems that happen to affect both of them.

What's wrong with that? Nothing. In fact, this suggestion seems to me to be the type of thing that the new referees' association should grab by the horns. I've always told Johnny Nucatola that the referees need a good rapport with the coaches, and, of course, the only way to establish that rapport is with communication. Let me amend that: with sensible communication.

Friday, January 18 (Chicago at Detroit)

I did not have the pleasure of communicating with Dick Motta during the Bulls-Pistons game tonight because Motta has been suspended for three games for communicating too much with the referees. Dr. Bob Biel, the Chicago trainer, coached the Bulls, but knowing Motta, I suspect he was hiding somewhere in the stands flashing hand signals, baseball-style, throughout the game.

Manny Sokol and I expected a rough game because the teams had engaged in several physical clashes during their last meeting. Then again, referees have learned to expect rough games routinely whenever the Bulls or the Pistons happen to be on the court. However, this was a relatively quiet game compared to their last donnybrook. The Pistons satisfied the home crowd by pulling away to victory at the end. However, I think the Bulls might have won the game if Jerry Sloan had not been ejected via the two-technical route. Early in the game Manny called an offensive foul on Sloan, then turned his back on the play. The irate Sloan raised the ball over his shoulder in a throwing motion, looking as though he intended to throw a fastball at the back of Manny's head. "Don't do it," I intoned. Sloan pulled the ball down, but then, before I could react, he whipped it down court at Sokol. He probably could have hit him if he had good aim, but he missed. Lucky for him. I called a technical foul, and I'm sure that he expected it. Gestures of disdain, such as firing a basketball at a referee, will always earn technicals.

Later in the game I noticed Sloan leaping from the Chicago bench, running toward center court and yelling something at Sokol. For a moment I though Sloan was entering the game as a substitute, because his warm-up jacket fell off his shoulders as he ran toward the center line. Then he retreated to the bench almost as fast as he had left it. But the next time Detroit scored another basket I saw Sloan do the same thing. I will not abide by that conduct, of course, so I called a technical on Sloan—and out he went. Then Chicago rallied to tie the Pistons near the end of the game, but the surge fizzled out. I, for one, think Sloan's presence might have had a more positive effect on the outcome of the game from a Chicago standpoint. As it turned out, Sloan wasn't there when his team needed him.

Saturday, January 19 (Sick Day)

Manny Sokol is what you'd call a true friend. I was not feeling well when I woke up in Detroit this morning. Once or twice each season I seem to come down with something called the Kasulkin Virus. Anyway, my throat is sore

(99)

and raspy and I feel slightly punch-drunk. So Manny volunteered to work for me tonight in Atlanta even though it meant he would have to miss a family wedding. At game time I was taking dosages of medication in Greenwich.

Tuesday, January 22 (Houston at New York)

After spending three days in bed, I feel like a pale, thin man. And who was the first person I saw tonight when I checked into the official's dressing room at Madison Square Garden? Mark Schlafman, wearing a sun-burned face and complaining that Miami was too hot over the weekend. The next time we have a blizzard I'm going to invite Schlafman to my place for a few days.

Houston beat New York, as Cliff Meely, a big forward, had a fantastic shooting game, probably the best exhibition of his brief NBA career. Basketball is mainly a game of match-ups, of course, and for some reason the Rockets and the Knicks offer two of the better *mano-a-mano* duels in basketball, featuring young Rudy Tomjanovich against old-hand Dave DeBusschere, and young Mike Newlin against cool Clyde Frazier. Tomjanovich is really the new DeBusschere, and when DeBusschere retires at the end of the season to become general manager of the New York Nets of the ABA, I suspect that Tomjanovich will begin to receive the recognition DeBusschere has earned as probably the best two-way forward in the game.

Tomjanovich, in fact, played DeBusschere so well in Houston's upset victory that I thought DeBusschere got a little frustrated. I even saw DeBusschere throw an elbow at Tomjanovich at one point. Not a vicious elbow, just one of those elbows that says: "Why can't I get away from this guy?" Then DeBusschere gave Tomjanovich a taste of his own tonic. Rudy was tired and about ready to go to the bench for a rest, but he had the ball as the Rockets moved down court. One of the surest things in basketball is that a player who knows he is coming out of the game, having seen his substitute on the sidelines, will fire up that one last shot for effect. DeBusschere, of course, knew this and, sure enough, he smash-blocked Tomjanovich's shot and set up an easy basket for the Knicks.

Newlin worked effectively against Frazier most of the game, and one time he made Clyde look bad by faking him completely out of the play and scoring an easy basket. Well, when Frazier gets burned, particularly on a one-on-one situation, he almost always goes head-to-head against the same player and tries to gain immediate revenge. So he dribbled down court against Newlin—and ten fakes later he found himself all alone under the basket for an easy 2 points. You could see Frazier looking over at Newlin and thinking: "Anything you can do, I can do better."

Newlin also was an innocent bystander of sorts in the one ugly incident that punctuated an otherwise quiet evening. On jump shots, many players tend to pitch their bodies forward after releasing their shot in an attempt to draw a foul on the defender. On this one play I was the lead referee, working under the basket as Newlin took a jump shot. After Newlin released the ball he made contact with a New York player, and Schlafman called a foul on the defender. I handled the execution of the foul, and as I was standing near the foul line, the New York bench—particularly Red Holzman, the coach, and Danny Whelan, the trainer—gave me a strong going over, claiming that Newlin had committed the foul, not the Knicks' player.

I listened to them, knowing that I wouldn't be standing there for more than a few seconds and, hell, referees are expected to take a few seconds of bitching every so often. Then we went down the floor, and this time Newlin committed a foul. There was no question about it, and I had to call it. However, in my mind, I almost didn't want to call it because I didn't want the Knicks to think they might have talked me into calling a foul. What's right is right, though, and I called the foul.

When I turned to the scorer's table to give Newlin's number, I noticed that I was getting a derisive round of applause from Whelan and some other Knicks. There was a foul shot awarded on the play, so as we were waiting for play to resume I called Holzman to my side. I warned him to maintain control over his bench—or else. Holzman claimed that Newlin had been tricking the referees all night.

"That's not what I'm here for," I told Holzman. "I'm here to tell you that your bench is out of control—and that you'd better control it, or else I will be forced to enforce the rules to the letter."

As I walked away, Holzman said: "I don't give a shit what you do." So I turned around and called a technical foul on him. That's what I had to do. You know, sometimes I say to myself: "Why the hell not go through the game casually and not try to control it?" Well, I have to—or else I won't be doing my job.

Remember. Every action creates a reaction. Coaches, for instance, should not be permitted to make that "Get out of my life" wave with their arms. If we tolerate that, we're only inviting trouble. I remember that night in Boston when John Havlicek asked me why I had reacted so violently to a particular action by some player. The individual had said something to me in a loud voice, so I had reacted in a loud voice. Listen. Ol' Double D doesn't want to be defeated on that basketball court. I counter with the same voice pitch that the player has just used on me. It's part of the professionalism of the official. At the same time, we must control ourselves and cannot overreact in any way.

Friday, January 25 (K.C.–Omaha at Buffalo)

Before they beat the Buffalo Braves tonight, several Kansas City–Omaha players told me that Nate Williams, one of the guards for the Kings, has been offered a football

(*102*)

contract by the Cincinnati Bengals of the NFL. Williams happened to be in Cincinnati recently and dropped by Riverfront Stadium to work out in the Bengals' exercise room. He started to fool around with the weights, and now it seems that he ranks No. 2, behind some Cincinnati tackle, in all weight-lifting categories on the Nautilus exercise machine. Nate's probably the strongest guard in the NBA, if not the strongest player at any position.

Tonight I worked with Lenny Wirtz, whom I had not seen since training camp more than four months ago. After the game we had a long dinner at the hotel and discussed, among other things, the new referees' association, of which I'm not a member. Why? Stated simply, I never want to be pressured by any group into making a decision about my career that might not be in my best personal interests. As far as I am concerned, refereeing in the NBA is a privilege —and not simply some right that can be bargained collectively. I hope my fellow referees understand my position, but whether they do or not, I know that off-court feelings have never interferred with the conduct of our jobs on the court.

Jake O'Donnell, the president of the referees association (actually, the group has no official name yet), and I have frequently debated the pros and cons of the organization. What will it do? How will it function? Most of the answers are unclear now. Basically, I guess what really bothers me most about the association is the implied threat by some members that "we won't work unless . . ." Unless what? Lenny is the treasurer of the association and a pretty good organizer, having learned the hard way, I'd say, by running the Ladies Professional Golf Tour for a number of years. I don't think even Henry Kissinger could get all those women to agree on anything at any one particular time.

Lenny also confirmed that what I had suspected all season was indeed true: teams do have pre-game meetings to discuss the officials working their game, and construct their game plan around the habits and idiosyncracies of the officials. In fact, Lenny said one player told him he played defense differently in every game, depending upon the referees. He knew what he could and could not get away with against certain officials, and played accordingly. Once again this puts the onus back on us. We must strive to be as consistent as we possibly can. There isn't any way for the league to instruct us as to judgment, but it can teach proper court position and help us work in closer accord with our partners. Above all else, we can't let players take advantage of us.

Sunday, January 27 (New York at Atlanta)

The trouble with working a television game is that you never know when the cameras or parabolic microphones will be pointed in your direction. Several weeks ago I happened to watch a Boston-Atlanta game on CBS and some of the things I heard over the air practically made me fall out of my chair. I had never realized how powerful the parabolic microphone really is. It represents another albatross to hang around the neck of the referee, because he knows that an entire country is capable of hearing what the players, the coaches and the trainers are saying to him. It's one thing to be called a son-of-a-bitch in private, but to be called a son-of-a-bitch with a few million people listening in is another matter. Referees will usually let a little foul language pass without notice. On the other hand, with the wonders of electronic engineering in operation, how can I let even the smallest profanity go by, when some kid in Bismarck, North Dakota, can hear every unprintable thing said on the court loud and clear?

In the Atlanta-Boston game the cameras and mikes were quick to pick up the reactions, both physical and verbal, of Tommy Heinsohn and Cotton Fitzsimmons throughout the game. Needless to say, the referees were on the receiving end. Both coaches looked as if they were competing for

Emmys, and their very visible and audible outbursts did nothing to enhance the reputation of the officials.

Today I'm working my first CBS game since I saw that zoo scene on television two weeks ago. And my partner is Mark Schlafman, who also happened to be one of the referees in that game. And, would you believe it? Atlanta happens to be one of the teams, squaring off against the New York Knicks. To complicate matters, certain frictions have recently developed between (1) Red Holzman and myself and (2) Mark Schlafman and Cotton Fitzsimmons. We're aware of the situation—and I know the coaches are, too.

The league office discussed the Holzman matter with me and they suggested that I personally assure Mr. Holzman that I was not carrying out a vendetta against him. Leaving the dressing room, I had no idea about what I would say to Mr. Holzman. I had even asked Johnny Nucatola for suggestions as to how I ought to broach the subject because this would be a career first for me. "Do it your own way, then it will end up right," Nucatola said.

So I went to Mr. Holzman minutes before the tap-off and asked if I could talk with him. He nodded his head. For some reason I then put my right hand on his left shoulder. "Red, I understand that there is a problem between the two of us, but I want you to know that my only ambition is to become the best referee ever. I've got nothing against you —or anyone else—in this business."

His response: "Richie, that's what I want to be, too. The best coach in the business."

Schlafman and Fitzsimmons had a brief discussion prior to the opening tap, too, but wouldn't you know that Mark had to eject Cotton soon after the game got underway?

I could tell in the early moments of the game that Fitzsimmons plainly doesn't like the way Schlafman officiates, and for the sake of professional basketball this irritant between them must be removed. It's too damn bad we can't sit down a couple of times a year and hash these things out.

The best way to eliminate problems and grievances is to air them fully.

Personally I know of no coach or player in the NBA who has carried a grudge for any length of time and still survived. There is no question that some referees have carried grudges, and to the credit of the NBA, the referees who have had that problem are discovered and quickly weeded out from the ranks. Others fall by the wayside because they don't have the ability to take abuse. Sure, abuse hurts, but you can't let it get to you.

New York won the game handily, and afterwards at the airport I bumped into the CBS crew at the Delta Airlines lounge. They said there hadn't been any language problems during the game. I asked Elgin Baylor if he had seen the replay of a walking violation I had called on Pete Maravich. On the play Maravich was driving down court, tried to go around Jerry Lucas, somehow got his foot tied up with Lucas' feet, and staggered past me for five or six off-balance, out-of control steps. Lucas, jarred by the impact, bumped into me. At this point there were three things I could have called: (1) offensive foul on Maravich; (2) blocking foul on Lucas; (3) a walking violation on Maravich. It seemed to me that walking was the only thing I could call with any certainty and that's what I did. When Maravich saw I had called him for walking, his mouth opened in surprise. He didn't say anything to me, but if he had, I'd have told him I didn't know *what* the hell to call. Elgin said they had replayed the incident, and he said he thought I had made the right call. Well, we win some of them anyway.

Tuesday, January 29 (Seattle at Houston)

The Houston players were strangely quiet during their loss to Seattle, except, that is, for Ron Riley, the big forward. After one call against the Rockets, Riley ran up to Bill Jones, my officiating partner, and had the misfortune to say the magic word, with the forseeable results. After the game an angry Riley came into our dressing room and demanded to know if Bill and I were going to listen to him. No way, when he's in that state of mind.

Riley left the room for a couple of minutes, and then returned in a much calmer mood. He wanted us to know that he might have said the magic word but he did not intend it for Bill Jones. Fine. We heard his explanation, and I will report it that way to the league office. I don't know what they'll do. Normally Riley is not an abusive player, and probably will develop into a great forward.

Wednesday, January 30 (Buffalo at Detroit)

Detroit may replace Philadelphia as my jinx town. I arrived here feeling super, but in less than eight hours I had another sore throat. Somehow I struggled through the game as the Pistons eased to a victory over the Buffalo Braves, with Bob Lanier hauling down every rebound in sight. At the end of the game I had a temperature of 101, and by the time I got back to Greenwich my temperature was 102-plus. Thank God I've got five days off before my next game. Maybe I'll be able to lose some weight, which I certainly could afford to do. With this sore throat, flu and rising temperature, I won't be touching the Double Ds. I won't even be having any Single Ds.

Tuesday, February 5 (Los Angeles at Houston)

Frankly, I've never been so depressed in my entire officiating career. What the hell is the game of basketball coming to? The games are turning into exhibitions of football, boxing, rugby, karate, and sumo wrestling. Everything except basketball.

My depression began early in the first quarter tonight,

when Jerry West, who had just returned to the Los Angeles line-up after several months on the sidelines with an assortment of injuries, tried to stop on the composition floor and damaged his left thigh for the umpteenth time. It was pathetic to see this great athlete limping painfully past me. Indeed, this may well be the last injury Jerry will ever suffer on a basketball court. He has talked of retirement recently, and when he left the court tonight there was a look on his face that clearly said, "God, what next?"

After West left the game, the action became very physical. Jim Price, who took West's place, drove down the lane and took a shot. When my eyes left Price to follow the play I heard someone yell, "Shit!" It was Price, as it turned out, and Tommy Nunez gave him a technical foul. Price was upset that neither Tommy nor I saw any foul on his missed shot. Moments later I was the lead referee, working under the basket, as Mike Newlin cut down the middle on a drive. Suddenly Price's left hand snaked out and grabbed Newlin's shirt. Newlin reacted by knocking Price's hand away. I promptly called a foul on Price for interfering with Newlin on the drive.

As we moved the other way again, Price and Newlin started to make menacing gestures, and began exchanging expletives.

"Gentlemen," I intoned, "the first man who closes his fist is gone."

Price jerked his head and said sarcastically, "Yeah, I thought you'd say something like that." Well, I didn't take well to that remark, of course, so I called his number.

"Oh, yeah, I thought so," Price answered in that same sarcastic tone.

By that, I think Price meant one of two things: (1) either I was favoring the home player—Newlin; or (2) I was favoring the white player—Newlin. Under no circumstances could I abide by his comment, so I called a technical on him. To my surprise, it was the second technical on Mr.

Price, so out he went. Now Price was the second Laker guard to leave the game.

Meanwhile, a nasty situation was developing between Happy Hairston of the Lakers and rookie forward E. C. Coleman of the Rockets. As we moved down the floor I called a foul on Hairston for knocking Coleman to the floor on a rebound. Then, as play went the other way, Coleman went by Hairston and gave him a shot in the solar plexus, and down went Hairston. Tommy and I both saw Coleman bowl Hairston over, but neither of us saw the punch to the solar plexus.

"Did you see an elbow or a fist?" I asked Nunez after he called the foul on Coleman.

"No," he answered.

Hairston was understandably irritated. Moments later, I called a foul on Hairston and he blew up. He gave me a disdainful gesture, waving his hands in disgust, and used a lot of profanity, and I called a technical foul. That should have warned Hairston, who has been around the NBA for many years, that I had heard enough for one night. However, after I called the technical, Hairston proceeded to tell me what to do with myself in no uncertain terms. Wearily, I signaled technical No. 2. Now the Lakers were minus three of their regular players.

Still, they rallied from behind and took a 3-point lead into the final minute. With 13 seconds left in regulation, Newlin missed a shot and the ball bounced away. The Lakers, wary of giving up a 3-point play, didn't charge for the ball. Houston missed another shot, but Rudy Tomjanovich got the rebound, shot it wildly and was hacked by Bill Bridges. Would you believe it? The ball went in. Bridges was understandably upset. It's one thing to foul a player in the closing minutes, but it's another thing to give that player a chance for a 3-point play when your team is leading by 3 points. There are good and bad fouls by the players' standards, and this was an example of a *very* bad foul.

Tomjanovich made the free throw, tying the game, and then the Rockets won in overtime. Did Bridges make a mistake? I frankly don't think so. Bill reacted to a situation that had developed, and it was just unfortunate that his reaction cost the Lakers the ball game. You can't start teaching players not to react.

After it was all said and done, Tommy and I retired to the dressing room for some peace and quiet. A nice hot shower, a couple of Double Ds, a good night's sleep—and everything would be forgotten. But the shower didn't work. Instead of gently spraying water, the shower head forces it out in a great, swooshing, jet-like stream. Cripes! Houston is the only place in the NBA where a referee can get ruptured while taking a shower.

The Coleman-Hairston conflict reminds me of two stories. One night years ago in St. Louis, Corky Devlin of the Pistons speared Cliff Hagan of the Hawks with an elbow, sending Hagan sprawling and knocking the wind out of him. Hagan, who was nicknamed "L'il Abner" for his unruffled manner, got off the deck and, in very definite terms, warned Devlin that he was going to get even. I happened to overhear Hagan's words, and said, "Cliff, if you get Devlin, Powers is going to get you."

"Richie," Hagan said, "you're not going to see me do it."

Early in the second half as I was running down the court I heard a gasp from the crowd that told me something awful had happened. I turned to my right and there was Devlin, flat on his back with his hands covering his face. Hagan was standing over him. "I told you I was going to get you," he said. I chased Hagan from the game, of course. What he had done was run up to Devlin at full tilt and lower the boom with a body block. Retribution, perhaps, but it was a terrible way to get even with someone. I went to Corky's side, and opened his fingers. His face looked like hamburger. It was as aggressive an act as I have ever seen.

Another time I was working a game between the Chicago Zephyrs or the Chicago Packers (who can remember the names of all the teams the NBA has had in Chicago?) and the Boston Celtics at the old International Amphitheatre out in the stockyards on Chicago's South Side. Boston had the ball and worked it in close to Clyde Lovellette, my old pre-game gunslinging rival. Wide Clyde took a hook shot and then, without a pause, took his left elbow and smashed it across the chest of Walt Bellamy, the big rookie center of the Chicago team. Have you ever heard a kettle drum? Strike the kettle drum once, listen to the reverberation, and that's what the result of Lovellette's well-placed elbow sounded like. Bellamy hardly flinched, though. He showed right there that he could take any punishment that the NBA had to offer.

Wednesday, February 6 (Boston at Milwaukee)

I called Ed Batogowski in Atlanta at the crack of dawn to check on his travel plans to Milwaukee for the Celtics-Bucks game tonight, and he told me there was a heavy snowstorm in the Midwest. Ed suggested that I fly from Houston to Atlanta and meet him there so we could attack Milwaukee together. I vetoed that proposal quickly. I said I would go through Chicago as planned, and I told him to start out from Atlanta. That way we couldn't get stranded somewhere together.

My flight from Houston to Chicago circled O'Hare Field for almost three hours before the control tower let the pilot try an instrument landing. The visibility was nil. I didn't see the runway until we were about ten feet over it. The guy who discovered radar ought to get a Nobel Prize twice a year. We touched down shortly after 2:00 P.M., about four hours late, and immediately called Johnny Nucatola in New York.

"How'd you get to Chicago?" he asked.

"I didn't walk here," I answered.

Johnny said that Batogowski was hung up somewhere

down south and probably would not make it to the game. However, Mark Mano, who lives in Racine, Wisconsin, called Nucatola earlier in the day to volunteer his services in case of emergency, and Johnny, in turn, suggested that Mark ought to drive to Milwaukee. I had to drive to Milwaukee, too. I rented a car at O'Hare and headed off into the snow. The Chicago-Milwaukee trip normally takes about seventy-five minutes. This afternoon it took almost four hours of the most hectic driving I can recall. Snow was blowing in swirls, the road was clogged with trucks, cars and tow trucks. I'm normally a cool driver, but I was so scared I began to perspire. I got hot and cold flashes. It was so bad that I didn't know whether to put on the heat or the air conditioning, to keep the windows open or closed.

I checked into my downtown motel at 6:30 P.M., less than ninety minutes before the start of the game. For a time I didn't think there would be a game, which would have been fine with me. I'd have given my right arm for just one Double D at that point. The Bucks had played last night in Kansas City, and they spent the entire day getting from Kansas City to Milwaukee. They took a flight to Minneapolis, caught a connection to Madison, Wisconsin, then bussed into Milwaukee. The Celtics, on the other hand, played last night in Chicago and took a leisurely post-game bus ride to Milwaukee before the snow had even begun to fall. Not surprisingly, the Bucks called Red Auerbach, the boss of the Celtics, and suggested that the game be postponed until tomorrow night. Can you guess what Auerbach said? The Celtics are scheduled to play the Knicks in Boston on Friday night, and there is no way Auerbach intends to have his team play the Bucks in Milwaukee one night and the Knicks in Boston the next. I can't blame him, either.

There was still no word from Batogowski, so Mano dressed and worked the game with me. The weary Bucks somehow managed to stay with the Celtics for three periods and, in fact, led by 10 points early in the final quarter. Then Dave Cowens gave a tremendous demonstration of ten-way basketball—rebounding, shooting, shot blocking, playmaking, you name it—and the Celtics rallied to scrape out a 1-point victory. I'll never forget one play Cowens made near the end. Don Chaney of the Celtics shot a free throw, but he missed, and the ball rolled off the rim toward Kareem Abdul-Jabbar. Before Jabbar could react, the red-headed streak named Cowens grabbed the ball, stuffed it and was gone. Cowens acted like a ghost who had just stolen the crown jewels.

By the way, do you think Milwaukee has great basketball fans? There were thirty inches of the white stuff on the ground, but the building was packed to the rafters. And not once did the crowd or the players get on the referees. The Bucks and the Celtics played basketball the way it was meant to be played. They could have played without a team of referees on the court. And that reminds me of something Dolly Stark, one of the great old referees, told me once. "Richie," he said, "the greatest accolade a referee can get is deadly silence." So I'd say that Mark and I received our greatest accolade tonight in snowy Milwaukee.

Friday, February 8 (New York at Boston)

The Milwaukee weather didn't do much for my physical condition. I spent the entire day yesterday nursing another cold.

This morning I flew to Boston for what I thought would be another classic Celtics-Knicks confrontation. What we had, instead, was another blowaway win for the Celtics, who absolutely chased the bedraggled Knicks out of the Boston Garden. Dave DeBusschere was injured early in the game which didn't help the New York cause. I don't think the Knicks would have won tonight's game if they had twelve DeBusscheres in their line-up.

After the game Ginger asked me if it was a good victory for Boston. All victories are good, to be sure, but this really was not a "good" victory for the Celtics. Experienced teams such as the Knicks—and the Celtics—never take a blowaway defeat very hard. They know they will lose by a big score a couple of times each season, and they condition themselves to expect those games. In fact, John Havlicek even said that the loss meant "nothing" to New York. The pros in the NBA want to win all the games they play, but they really want to win the close contests. They're the big morale boosters, or morale lowerers, depending where you happen to wind up. It's easy to forget a 30-point defeat, but it's not so easy to forget a 1-point defeat in overtime. Those are the games that linger and linger and linger.

Saturday, February 9 (Philadelphia at Capital)

The new Capital Centre in Landover, Maryland, is a spectacular arena except for one thing. The clocks don't work. They spent $50 million to build the place, but can't get the clocks going. So now they have to superimpose the clock on the four 20-by-15-feet television screens hanging over center court. Other than that, the building is fabulous. It has everything a player, an official or a fan could ever need. Even the showers work.

The Bullets plan to show instant replays on the overhead screens, but they won't be flashing any replays of controversial situations involving referees, just spectacular scoring plays, defensive maneuvers and rebounding action. My hat is off to the Bullets' management. They know that instant replays focusing on officials will only lead to trouble. Besides, referees never make mistakes.

The replay machine was overworked during the game as the Bullets jumped to a quick 25-point lead over the Philadelphia 76ers and went on to rout them by more than 35 points. It was my first experience working a game with a replay machine. On one play Phil Chenier of the Bullets faked out a Philadelphia player and threw in a twisting jumper. The crowd roared appreciatively. Then, seconds later, as the 76ers were passing the ball around, the crowd roared again when the replay was shown. It's going to take a little getting used to.

Sunday, February 10 (Capital at Philadelphia)

Capital-Philadelphia again, this time at the Spectrum in my jinx city. Again, Capital jumped to an early lead but, unlike last night, the Bullets never applied the killing pressure when they had the 76ers in distress. So Philadelphia kept rallying and then, at the end, Freddy Carter connected on two jumpers, and led the 76ers to a 2-point victory.

Despite the closeness of the score, it was a relatively easy game to officiate. We had only one disputed call, when I had to overrule Bill Jones. I was the trail referee on the play, while Jones was working under the basket. According to the referee's rule book, the lead referee controls the play when the ball is inside the foul line or near the sidelines, while the trail official handles everything deep. But this rule applies only to conflicting interpretations of the same play. Kevin Porter of the Bullets had been dribbling the ball, and Carter was behind him. When Porter stopped, Carter batted the ball out of his hands. Porter recovered the ball and began to dribble again. Bill Jones called his whistle to give a double-dribble call on Porter, but I waved my arms and told Bill that I was taking over the play. Bill had been blocked out slightly, so I walked over to him and explained the situation as I had seen it. He nodded his head in agreement, and that was that.

I think I must be mellowing. In the last four games I haven't called one technical foul.

Tuesday, February *12* (Phoenix at Portland)

Think referees haven't made any social progress in the last twenty years? People used to ignore us in the old days, figuring that we were a necessary evil, I guess, but certainly not deserving of any recognition other than constant boos and cat calls. Well, so far this season *Sports Illustrated* has done a major story on basketball referees, CBS-TV has done a video takeout on us, *Sport Magazine* has focused a probing story on us, and, most revealing, newspapers everywhere are spelling our names correctly. Powers may be an easy name, but they're even getting Batogowski, Mihalak and Schlafman right these days.

On top of all that, Ted Green of the *Los Angeles Times* will spend a week with me here on the West Coast so that he can write a story about the life and times of an NBA official. The *Los Angeles Times,* no less. When I came into the NBA, Los Angeles wasn't even in the league. I arrived here late last night, spent a good twelve hours in bed, and then met Ted for a late-afternoon snack.

"What does it take to be a good referee?" Ted asked as we waited for the club sandwiches.

"Beats the hell out of me," I said. "No one thinks *any* referee is good. To be good means being firm, decisive, unflappable and unshakable. I feel the game rests on my shoulders. And I know I will keep the game under control."

"What about the travel?"

"I don't like the road any better than anyone else," I said. "I'm always thinking about the wasted hours between games. That's why I always keep the television set turned on in my room. It's noise, but it's also companionship. I watch it until I get relaxed. It takes me three hours after a game to unwind. I look at the TV but most of the time I'm not really watching it."

I told Ted I read at least one book each week during the season, then I showed him my required reading for this week: *KGB,* a story about Russian spies. "I'm not so sure about this one," I said. "I've just read the flap, and I may not get past the first chapter.

Green rode out to the Portland Coliseum with Ed Batogowski and me, and stayed in the dressing room during our regular pre-game meeting. Ed and I discussed the possibility that it might be a rough game, mainly because the two centers, Neal Walk of Phoenix and Rick Roberson of Portland, like to play physically and because Sidney Wicks of Portland usually gets so involved in the game that he sometimes loses his temper. Besides that, both teams happened to be on losing streaks, so they probably would stop at nothing in order to get a victory.

"Do you always have meetings like this?" Green asked.

"I do, yes," I said. "However, some referee tandems don't pool their info beforehand, and I think it hurts them. Was there a fight the last time these teams played? Did one player eat up another? Is anyone trying anything new lately? You know, it takes awhile for word to get around that one player likes to grab guys by the pants so they can't move, or that another likes to pull guys down on top of him to make it look like an offensive foul. Tonight, for instance, we will be keeping a close eye on Dick Van Arsdale of the Suns. He's such an intense competitor that he doesn't see the people he runs over and can't believe he has been called for a foul even when they're picking up the guy with a blotter."

Predictably, the trouble began with the first call—or noncall. One of the Phoenix players tossed up a fifteen-foot jumper and Wicks easily batted the ball away. It was a legal block, no doubt about it. Behind me I heard some verbiage from the area of the Phoenix bench. I thought to myself that it was a little early for flak, but, then again, this year it seems that the first call of a game is always questioned. I turned and looked toward the Suns' bench, but saw nothing except a lot of closed mouths. Moments later, after I had turned my back to the Phoenix bench, I heard the same voices. Listen, if you want to talk to me, talk to my face, not my back. I looked over at the bench with a glare that told them I had had enough already. Right then John McLeod, the Phoenix coach, called a time out. "Richie," he said, "don't tell me I'm not going to be able to talk to you tonight." I reminded Mr. McLeod that the rules stipulate that a coach cannot talk to an official at any time, but we do allow coaches to confer with us if they do it in a gentlemanly fashion. There is no way we expect coaches to gag themselves completely. At the same time, we don't want them talking behind our backs.

When play resumed, Van Arsdale took the ball and drove aggressively toward the basket without looking at the obstacles in his path. Bernie Fryer of the Trail Blazers was one of those obstacles, and he ended up on the seat of his pants. I called an offensive foul on Van Arsdale, and he proceeded to play to form, by arguing loudly.

"Offense?" he yelled. "What kind of shit is that, Richie?"

I promptly signaled T to the scorer's table. Van Arsdale kicked his feet a couple of times. And then suddenly McLeod appeared at center court to act in Van Arsdale's defense.

"What kind of crap is that, Richie?" McLeod demanded.

"That's a T—and you'll have to return to your bench," I said.

"Horseshit!" McLeod said. "Go ahead and call your crappy T's."

"That's two T's now," I said. Exit John McLeod.

Why McLeod acted so volatilely is beyond me. Forget that stuff about basketball games being a vacation. After four games with no technical fouls, Ed and I handed out four in the first half. Then came the third period. Mike Bantom, a rookie with the Suns, drove down the lane and tossed up a shot. The ball did not go in, and Bantom thought he had been fouled in the act of shooting. Neither Ed nor I saw any foul, so we didn't call one. "Horseshit!" Bantom screamed. I blew my whistle and signaled another T.

Bantom was back on the Phoenix bench a few minutes later, and when I ran past him he yelled: "Hey, Powers, don't you call anything but technical fouls." I walked back to the Phoenix bench and said calmly: "That's your second technical, now disappear!" That surprised Bantom, but I considered his remark abrasive, totally unsportsmanlike, not to mention surly, sarcastic and snide. So the education of an NBA rookie continues: I doubt that Mr. Bantom will talk so strongly to any more referees. At least I hope not.

Portland scored 15 straight points down the stretch to break open a close game and beat the Suns handily. Back in the dressing room Ted Green expressed astonishment at some of the things he had seen on the court. "Tell me, Richie," he asked, "do players always argue so seriously when the infractions are so obvious?" All I could do was smile and shake my head. "In the old days, even last year," I said, "players seemed to accept the calls without great debate. But now every whistle is like a signal for a meeting of the local chowder and marching society. It seems to me that the players want to challenge our wills." I told Ted that this type of thinking must be stopped, or else the game would suffer serious consequences. I have talked to Johnny Nucatola about this.

Back at the hotel Ted joined Ed and me for a few drinks, and later he asked Ed how he enjoyed the life of a referee. "Some kind of life, huh?" Ed said. "People ask me when my daughter was born, and I say 'Philadelphia at Milwaukee.' When I look back, if one of my four kids has any problems, I invariably link them with the time I'm spending away from home. I just hope my wife is strong enough. Why do I do it? It's not the money. Sometimes I say to myself: Why am I taking all this crap? What am I proving? I guess it's the insatiable urge to be the best. I want to be as good as Richie or Mendy Rudolph. But, if the players continue to moan on every call, if they won't let me do it, I suppose I'll have to quit."

It was shortly after midnight when we headed for our

rooms. Ted walked the hotel corridor with me, and we were still chatting when I put the key into the lock and opened the door to my room. The television was on. "Companionship," I said. "It's like having someone to come home to."

Actually, it was *The Maltese Falcon*—and I have seen the movie about eight dozen times.

Wednesday, February 13 (off-day)

On the flight from Portland to Oakland this morning Ted asked why I thought there was so much complaining after every call made by a referee. "Maybe it's because we have a lot of young officials," I said. "Whatever it is, it has become a real vendetta in some cases. It doesn't bother me, though, because I know I'm a good referee. Still, I've got to admit that it's a general pain in the ass." Some coaches, I explained, are exploders, like Dick Motta and Tommy Heinsohn. He asked me about Bill Sharman of the Lakers. "Sharman snipes at you as you run past him," I said. "You don't think he got that bad voice by singing in a church choir, do you?" (This was meant jokingly, as Bill has been suffering from a throat infection for almost two years.)

I told Ted that most players fall into broad categories of bitching: there are the grunters, like Jerry Lucas; the gesturers, like Rick Barry; and the polite con-men, like Walt Bellamy. Bellamy likes to speak about himself in the third person. "Walter didn't foul," he'll say. Or, "Walter never gets a break." One night Norm Drucker had had enough of Bellamy's talks with himself, and after a flagrant violation of the rules he looked up at the Atlanta giant and said, "Will you please inform Walter that I am awarding him a technical foul?"

Since we had the night off I spent most of the afternoon sleeping in my room, and was right in the middle of a great sleep when Bob Ryan called me on the phone. Ryan normally covers the Celtics for the Boston *Globe*, but he happened to be on the Coast covering both the Celtics and the Boston Bruins this week. He wanted to know if I wanted to see the Bruins-California Golden Seals game with him. Can you imagine waking a basketball referee up on an off-day to ask him if he wants to see a hockey game? Ryan later joined the three of us—Green, Batogowski and me—in the hotel coffee shop.

Bob is one of the best, if not the best young basketball writer in the country. He knows the game, the players and the officials. This season, though, he has given the referees a pretty tough time in print. Personally, I think he has been too subjective. On the whole he has been good to me, although he did say I had worked a few bad games. Baloney. I don't allow myself the privilege of having bad games. Some games just are more difficult to control. I told Bob and Ted, "Listen. Anytime a referee says, 'I've had four good games and one bad one,' what he means is that he had one game that was poorly played—not poorly refereed." It was a good discussion, something we ought to have more of. In fact, when Ryan left us to go to his hockey game, Batogowski said to me: "Gee, I never thought that Bob was so intelligent about the game."

Thursday, February 14 (Atlanta at Golden State)

Just before Ed and I left our dressing room Ted Green asked me an odd question. "Do ever you think about the calls you make during a game?" Well, I had to think about that for a moment. "No," I said. "Once the game is started, I seem to have the facility to make instantaneous decisions." End of answer.

Out on the court Ed and I conducted the traditional pre-game meeting with the captains, Lou Hudson of the Hawks and Nate Thurmond of the Warriors. After it was over and we began to walk away Hudson called us back. "I forgot something," he said. "Cotton doesn't want you guys talking to us or to him during the game." I had heard that the Atlanta team was trying this approach, but it was my first encounter with the Hawks since Fitzsimmons decided to strike his blow for a conversational blackout. Batogowski looked at Hudson and said, "Fine, Lou. But remember, it's a two-way street. You don't talk to us, either."

The game was close at the half, and as Ed and I walked to the dressing room Fitzsimmons stopped me. "Richie, I want you to tell Batogowski not to talk to me." I asked Cotton what Ed had said to him. "He warned me," Cotton said and turned and stalked away. In the room I told Batogowski what Fitzsimmons had just said. "I just warned the man," Ed said.

I said, "Ed, I don't care what you said to him. He doesn't want you talking to him, therefore don't bother warning him. If he gets on you about a call, hit him with a technical. If he wants to be that way, apply the rules as strictly as you can."

Here's the point: referees do bend the rules. The warning we give to coaches isn't mentioned in the rulebooks, but we issue them as a preventive measure. If Cotton doesn't want a warning, then he's looking for trouble—and he'll get it. I spent part of the intermission period diagraming an out-of-bounds play on the wash basin mirror with a bar of soap. There had been some confusion on a play, and I wanted to refamiliarize Ed with the standard operating procedure on this sort of situation.

What happened was that Ed hadn't seen an out-of-bounds violation and asked me to call the play. I had seen the play and gave the ball to Golden State. Before the Atlanta players could react, the Warriors fired the ball down court for an easy layup basket. In the old days we always used to blow our whistle when the ball changed hands on in-bounds plays in order to alert the other team that play was about to resume. We don't do it now because the rules have been changed. I, for one, think we should blow the whistle on such plays and, in fact, I do blow my whistle at times. Still, the league office has warned me about this.

Atlanta was burned up about the quick basket. They had called time and Lou Hudson ran over. "Richie, what's the matter?"

"Nothing," I answered.

"Shouldn't it have been a jump ball?" Hudson asked.

"No," I said. "My partner didn't know what happened, but I saw it completely."

Hudson protested that the ball had hit Rick Barry of the Warriors on the way out of bounds. "If it hit Barry, then I missed the call," I said. "But the last guy I saw touch the ball was Jim Washington. If I'm wrong, I'm wrong—and it's too late to do anything about it."

Then Cotton Fitzsimmons walked over and, violating his vows of silence, asked "Hey, what happened?"

I told him what I had just told Hudson. Fitzsimmons countered with Hudson's story, that the ball had bounced out of bounds off Rick Barry.

"If it did," I said, "I missed it. But I didn't see it that way. I called what I saw."

We expected trouble from the Hawks in the second half, and, sure enough, trouble came right away. Ed called a foul on one of the Hawks and Fitzsimmons yelled: "Call them the same at both ends!" It was a routine comment at best, something that is said at least twenty or thirty times during a game, and something that referees have learned to expect from aggrieved coaches and players. However, hearing Fitzsimmons' comment, Batogowski did not hesitate a second to call a technical on the Atlanta coach. Then John Brown, the fine Atlanta rookie from the University of Missouri, mumbled something. "Young man," I growled, "if I can't talk to you, I'll be damned if you can talk to me." Still, there I was talking to a player.

I, for one, don't agree with the thinking behind the talking rule in the books. There can be, and there should be, meaningful dialogue in a game. If a player asks a referee why he called a foul, and asks the question with respect, the referee should have the opportunity to describe .he violation. Talking about describing things, Ted Green told me he particularly liked the manner in which I called a foul on Pete Maravich when he made contact with Rick Barry on one play. "Maravich, forty-four, you *yanked* Barry," I had intoned.

Hey, if someone commits a foul, why not tell the player what he did?

Friday, February 15 (Seattle at Los Angeles)

The Lakers set an NBA record by making 43 turnovers tonight, and I don't mean lemon and raspberry turnovers. On the other hand, the SuperSonics didn't know what to do with it when they got it. They took 113 shots, an extraordinary number for a 48-minute game, and connected only 42 times, a terrible percentage. "We didn't deserve to win the game," Bill Russell lamented after the Lakers somehow survived their largesse and beat his SuperSonics.

One thing I really like about Russell the coach, and definitely admired about Russell the player, is that he never blames the referees for the mistakes his players make. And he doesn't want his players blaming the referees for their blunders, either. For instance, on one play tonight I called a routine goal-tending on John Hummer of the SuperSonics and received some pretty strong verbal flak from Hummer in return. He argued so sternly that I said: "John, if I missed it, I'm sorry, but it looked pretty flagrant." Hummer was still protesting loudly as play moved down court, and both Russell and his assistant coach, Emmette Bryant, were off the Seattle bench. "Stop it, John, stop it!" Russell scolded. "It was a good call." So Hummer stopped humming.

After the game Batogowski asked me about the goal-tending play. He said he didn't think the ball would have hit the rim.

"How the hell do you know?" I said. "The ball was stopped before it reached the rim." I asked him what the rulebook said about goal-tending.

"The ball must have a reasonable chance," he answered.

"Right," I said. "Did that shot have a reasonable chance?"

"Yes."

"Period."

You can't project things back past infinity or something. That's assinine.

At times I think Ed gets too analytical about his calls. In basketball the referee has to let the chips fall where they may. If you see it, call it. Do it now. Don't examine in depth the reason you're calling it. Call it—and be done with the damn thing. Don't think this is an impersonal attitude for a referee to take, because it's not. It's a professional attitude. Call what happens! Period. Remember, problems start after a call—not before it. If a referee wonders whether or not he should call a foul, then he'll probably blow it and end up in a lot of trouble. Decisiveness is the strongest and most enduring quality a referee can have.

Ed seems to be having some troubles with his toss-ups on this trip. Think the game of basketball isn't getting pre-snickety when referees have to worry about how they throw the ball up between two giants on tap-off plays? Many years ago wise Red Auerbach counseled me on the need for making a proper and perfect toss on the tap-offs. "Think of it this way," Auerbach said. "The toss-up should serve as the foundation for what you want to build, and if you don't make the toss properly, then the foundation will not be built properly—and maybe the game will fall all around you." Red always used to yell at me "Start it right! Start it right!" when I was getting set to throw the ball in the air.

And I practiced the toss-up, too.

When you toss the ball into the air you can't give it any

side spin that might make the ball favor one of the players in the jump circle. I practiced a nice, firm underhanded motion, trying to create a soft, floating knuckleball. I also practiced getting out of the way of the giants as they flailed after the ball.

Another thought. If a referee makes a bad toss that favors one team, and that team happens to score an easy basket, well that's *really* a turnover. If a referee happens to make that mistake late in the game, hell, it could cost a team dearly. Coaches are absolutely right when they say that toss-ups are a terribly important matter.

Ted Green said good-bye after the game. Before leaving, he asked me what I was trying to do in the NBA. "Conquer Everest," I told him. "Every night is Everest. I don't have to go to Nepal to climb the damn mountain. It's in L.A., New York, Detroit, Boston, Atlanta—every night of the season. This job is damn near impossible. But I never wanted to do anything but what I'm doing now. Never. It's a thrilling vocation, even though I know 'thrilling' may be a silly word for a grown man to use. But what the hell. That's how I feel. I'm a jock. I like the world of basketball. And I get a charge out of being a pseudo-celebrity. Ted, I don't think you'd be interviewing me for five days if I were a plumber."

I think, I hope, that Ted understands some of the problems that confront a referee in the NBA.

Saturday, February 16 (Off-day)

Another off-day on the road, dammit! Since there was nothing better to do in Phoenix, I took a busman's holiday and watched the Atlanta-Phoenix game from a seat in the stands. It was awful. Not the game itself, but watching the game from the stands. I was too far away from the action to enjoy it, even though I was probably only twenty-five rows from the court. Sitting there I thought about how tough it must be for men like Sid Borgia who have to sit in the stands and make observations about the quality of the work being done on the floor by the referees. They—the observers, that is—don't know what the players are saying to the referees, or what the referees are saying to the players. They have a completely different view of the action on the court. And how, for that matter, can they watch both referees simultaneously? They can't.

What I really discovered, though, is that the normal tendency is to forget the referees and watch the game itself. Mendy Rudolph and Jim Capers worked the game. I could always predict where Mendy would be during a play because he's always in the right place at the right time. However, I had never seen Capers in action, except, of course, the few times we have worked together, and I wanted to study his movements. But, I got so involved in the game that I forgot about the referees.

A suggestion: I think the NBA should assign a *team* of observers to scout the referees. The observers could sit in different places for different quarters and get different views of the efficiency or inefficiency of the referees. And they could compare their notes after the game. Sure, it would be an expensive proposition, dollar-wise, but why not? The NBA is getting bigger and bigger every year, and the quality of the refereeing must be maintained at a peak level.

Sunday, February 17 (Portland at Phoenix)

After sitting around the hotel pool for a couple of hours this afternoon, and having nothing better to do, I watched the televised hockey game between the Philadelphia Flyers and the Montreal Canadiens. Game? It was a war. There were so many penalties that the scorer lost track of the minutes, and there were so many fights that the poor officials spent half the game separating combatants.

I was fascinated as I watched the referee handle the game. I think he did a spectacular job. He adjudicated the penalties and the ejections perfectly, and thanks to the referee—and only the referee—the third period was played in peace. Now I'm more and more convinced that hockey-style penalties are something that must become part of basketball. For certain basketball infractions, a player should be put into a penalty box or put on the bench or even sent to his dressing room for a period of time. What type of infractions? Profanity, for instance. In fact, any time a player chooses to excoriate a referee he should be given such a penalty. In other words, the players should be punished punitively, not just financially. If a player calls me a "Shithead," then he would be sent off the court for, say, six minutes. If he says it again, he gets another six minutes. Then, if he chooses to call me a "Shithead" for the third time, he should be ejected from the game completely. The hell with the fines. Money doesn't mean anything to basketball players these days. Do you think a $50 or $100 fine bothers a guy who's making a couple of hundred thousands dollars a year. The average salary in the NBA is around $100,000; $50 is something the players use to tip shoeshine boys and waiters.

And while I'm on the subject, do you know that one of Wilt Chamberlain's proudest boasts is that he never fouled out of a game during his distinguished NBA career? Some people insisted that the referees protected Chamberlain once he was in the slightest bit of foul trouble. Absolutely not! Chamberlain never fouled out because he realized he would be useless to his team sitting on the bench. I worked many games when Chamberlain had five fouls on him but refused to commit a sixth by avoiding any contact whatsoever with an opposing player. He would let the player go, rather than risk drawing the foul that would send him from the game. Right or wrong, I don't know. And I don't care. All I know is that Chamberlain never fouled out because he would never let himself foul out. Listen. We don't protect anyone on the court.

The game was Portland-Phoenix again, and Ed Batogowski and I worried that it might become a repeat of the mayhem that had transpired in Portland earlier this week. As we watched the teams complete their warm-ups, Batogowski overheard a remark Clem Haskins made to Mike Bantom of the Suns. "Hey, there's Powers," Haskins said to Bantom. "How long do you think he'll let you stay in the game tonight?" Bantom had to laugh. As it turned out, Bantom fouled out with only a couple of minutes to play in the final quarter.

Unlike the game up north, this was a quiet contest. Phoenix pulled to an early lead and maintained a good margin to the end. Late in the third quarter I received one of the biggest surprises of my life. I was administering a foul at the line when I heard a buzz from the stands. I looked at the scoreboard, the roof and the baskets in an attempt to find out what was causing the commotion. Everything was in working order, though, so the commotion obviously had nothing to do with us. Something must be happening in the crowd, probably a fight. Then one of the teams called a time out, and as the Suns walked to their bench Keith Erickson yelled to me and pointed to a group of fans stretched out at the far end of the court. I looked and saw that everyone was laughing. There in living color, with green-script writing against a brilliant yellow background, was a 4-by-40-foot banner with the words: "Throw Powers to the People!" I stepped to my left in order to get a good view of the banner, and then I broke up. I motioned to the man who had apparently made the sign, signaling that I'd like to have it. I pointed to him, then jerked my thumb over my shoulder saying, "Can I take it home with me?" The man nodded. Then I suddenly thought: Cripes! Maybe the guy thinks I want to meet him in the alley and have a fight.

When the quarter ended Jerry Colangelo, the general

manager of the Suns, asked me if I really wanted to take it home with me. "Of course," I said. So the fans rolled the banner back up and brought it to the dressing room at the end of the game.

It was a funny scene. I was as gracious as I could possibly be and thanked them profusely for letting me have the banner. Perhaps my reaction disarmed them. Perhaps they thought I'd get angry. Hell, no. As fans, they have a right to do such things as long as they remain within their bounds during the playing of the game. These fans were not on the floor, and they did not intrude on the game. They just put up a sign. Great! I had no animosity toward them. And, as I told them, despite what the people in Phoenix might think, I did not break the rules in Portland. The Phoenix players did. And they paid the price with their technical fouls.

I'll be home in Greenwich tomorrow, and the first thing I'll do is hang the banner in the den. Throw Powers to the People. Right on!

Wednesday, February 20 (Golden State at K.C.–Omaha)

How's this for an intriguing schedule for all you people who think that flying around the country is one big Double D excursion on a 747 with movies and good-looking stewardesses and plenty of time to catch up on your beauty rest: Omaha on Wednesday, Toronto Thursday, Chicago Friday, New York Saturday, Cleveland Sunday, Greenwich Monday, Detroit Tuesday, and Atlanta on Wednesday. Seven games in eight nights. Join the NBA and see the U.S.A.

For the rest of the schedule I probably will be working with older, experienced officials more often than I have in recent months. As the playoffs draw closer, and with teams fighting for playoff position, the league generally tries to protect itself by assigning the more experienced referees to the more important games. Personally, I don't understand this thinking, because these games should be no more important than the games played in October, November, December and January. As far as I am concerned, they're all tough. Some games may be "big" for some players some of the time. But every game is a "big" game for us.

By big-game standards, I suppose that the Warriors–Kings game tonight in Omaha was a "big game" for Golden State, which is battling Los Angeles for first place in the Pacific Division. The way the playoffs are structured the division champions in both conferences automatically earn a playoff berth but the two remaining spots in each conference will be awarded to the teams with the best record. With Detroit and Chicago both playing strong basketball in the Midwest Division, it appears that only the winner of the Pacific Division will qualify for the playoffs. Golden State presently leads the Lakers by a hair in the standings, but the Warriors missed a golden opportunity to increase their lead tonight when they were routed by Kansas City–Omaha. Don Kojis and Nate Williams handled the Kings' scoring, and big Sam Lacey dominated the boards as the Warriors had to play without the injured Nate Thurmond once again. The real sparkplug for the Kings, though, was a kid I don't think I had ever seen play basketball before; rookie guard Mike D'Antoni from Marshall University. He was everywhere on the court, setting up plays, stealing the ball, popping in jump shots and directing the K.C.–Omaha attack flawlessly. I was not the only person in Omaha who was unfamiliar with Mr. D'Antoni.

"Who the hell is that kid?" one of the Warriors asked me after D'Antoni stole the ball and went in for a 3-point play. The name is D'Antoni.

Thursday, February 21 (New York–Buffalo at Toronto)

If Philadelphia is my jinx city, then I must be the jinx referee for the New York Knickerbockers. For the third time in recent weeks I handled a game in which the Knicks were absolutely blown out by the opposition. The Buffalo Braves shot better than 70 percent in the first half, better than 60 percent in the second and thoroughly dominated the Knicks for 48 minutes. The Knicks claim they do not regard these blowout contests as real defeats, but I'm sure that Coach Red Holzman is beginning to wonder why the Knicks have been losing so many blowouts in the past few weeks. Dave DeBusschere passed off the rout by calling it a "good workout."

The best thing about blowout games for the referees is that the games usually are mild, peaceful affairs in which the prevailing attitude of the players on both teams seems to be "let's get it over with quickly." I called Ginger when I returned to my hotel near the Toronto airport and asked her if she had watched the game on television. "For a quarter," she said. I couldn't really blame her for switching to the Thursday night movie instead.

Friday, February 22 (Portland at Chicago)

I knew I was in trouble when the Toronto weatherman reported that it was the warmest February 22 in the city's history. It was about 55 degrees outdoors, the sun was shining and people were strolling around in sweaters instead of parkas. All things considered, I was very cheerful as I stepped up to the check-in counter at the airport and presented my ticket for the Toronto-to-Chicago flight. "Sorry, sir," the girl said, "Chicago is closed because of bad weather and most likely will be closed all day." So I did what I always do when confronted with trouble: I called Johnny Nucatola in New York. "You can't be in Toronto," Nucatola said. "You're supposed to be in Chicago." I told him I was stuck because Chicago was closed, but that I'd try some finagling. My Chicago flight was canceled, and I thought about driving a rent-a-car to Buffalo, about two hours away, and trying to get into Chicago from there, but if Chicago was closed, it was closed.

At noontime the reservations girl told me they expected Chicago to open around 4:00. Great! "Get me a seat on the three-thirty flight," I said. She looked at me quizzically and then said, "Have you looked outside recently, sir?" I hadn't, as a matter of fact, and when I did I couldn't believe my eyes. The day that had started with beautiful summer-type weather had disintegrated into a typical wintery Toronto day, with heavy snow falling and swirling in gusty winds. I called Nucatola again to report on my lack of progress. He said that Jim Capers and Lee Jones were flying to Chicago from Houston and that Tommy Nunez was stuck in Chicago because of the bad weather. So no matter what happened to me, the NBA was protected.

Still, I had to try to get to Chicago. I kept running back and forth between terminals, checking on flights west. Toronto-to-Winnipeg-to-Chicago was a possibility. So was Toronto-to-Windsor, limousine from Windsor to Detroit and jet from Detroit to Chicago. One smart-aleck ticket agent suggested that I take the 1:30 P.M. flight from Toronto to San Francisco and then catch the 5:00 P.M. San Francisco-Chicago flight. In the end, I took a flight that was bound for Acapulco but had to make an unscheduled stop in Chicago to pick up some passengers that were stranded because of the poor weather earlier in the day. The only bad thing about the flight was that all the other passengers were heading for vacationland and quickly began to unwind over a couple of drinks. All I could do was to sit there with a cup of coffee and get ready to work a basketball game.

Once in Chicago I called Nucatola for the third time. "Where are you now?" he asked. "Kalamazoo?"

"Would you believe Chicago?" I said.

The game? Chicago beat Portland. It was the easiest part of the day. After the game I took another cab back to the airport and caught the 11:00 P.M. flight back to New York. I arrived in Greenwich at 3:30 A.M. Not surprisingly, no one in the family was awake to greet me at the door. So I made a lot of noise opening the door, dropping my luggage, bumping into a wall and toppling a chair. That woke them up.

Saturday, February 23 (Atlanta at New York)

Tommy Nunez was understandably nervous as we sat around our dressing room before the start of the Hawks-Knicks game tonight. It was Tommy's first game at Madison Square Garden, and don't let anyone ever tell you there isn't something different about working your first game in the Garden. The league office is in the adjacent office tower at Penn Plaza, of course, and Big Brother no doubt is watching you. By Big Brother, I mean either Walter Kennedy, commissioner of the league, or Johnny Nucatola—or both. I left Tommy alone with his thoughts. I didn't attempt any bad jokes to ease his nervousness. I knew he'd come back to earth the minute he blew his whistle for the first time in the game.

I love working at the Garden except for one thing: the smoke. The Garden has a terrible exhaust problem, consequently the smoke hovers in a cloud bank over the floor, fogging things pretty badly. It's a problem, not just for the referees but for the players as well. I always seem to be fighting for my breath—and my eyes always seem to be on fire.

The Atlanta–New York game was fairly quiet, and Nunez comported himself beautifully. At halftime, though, we both got a scare when one of New York City's finest came running over as we were picking our warm-up jackets off the bench. Cotton Fitzsimmons was shocked, too. None of us knew what was happening. Had there been a bomb scare? A fire? The officer explained he was there to escort us to our dressing room. Just what I had always wanted: a police escort.

(*134*)

At halftime I learned the reason for the security build-up. It seems that earlier in the week an exuberant spectator in Milwaukee threw a cup of cold beer in the face of referee Don Murphy as he walked off the court following a Bucks defeat. Murphy accepted the foamy facial without protest, but when the fan proceeded to put up his dukes Don proceeded to lower the boom on the thirsty spectator with a single punch. For now on I'll call Murph "Old One-Punch."

While Atlanta was able to stay with the Knicks for the first half, they succumbed to New York's relentless defensive pressure in the second half and lost badly. After the game Ginger and I had dinner with Pete and Muriel Williams over at Jimmy Weston's place on 54th Street. Pete's a golf nut with a two-stroke handicap, and he kept picking up steak knives to demonstrate his new interlocking grip. Sure, Pete. But I much prefer the overlapping grip on a glass filled with my favorite post-game relaxant. I've never shanked a glass filled with Double D.

Sunday, February 24 (Phoenix at Cleveland)

I spent a month today in Cleveland. After getting to bed at 3:00 A.M., I got up at 5:45 to catch the 7:45 flight from New York. We landed in a blizzard, naturally, and by the time I reached the hotel it was practically noon. I spent the afternoon in bed, alternately sleeping, reading and watching the tube. I worked the Cleveland-Phoenix game with Tommy Nunez, who once again handled himself with perfection, and afterwards I jumped into a cab and instructed the driver to take me to a good restaurant. "Sorry, sir," the man said. "Everything's closed in Cleveland on Sunday night." I couldn't even get a sandwich, not even at McDonald's or Burger King or Burger Chef or Burger Bun or Burger Bits. Well, I guess I can afford to lose a few pounds. A *few*.

Tuesday, February 26 (Boston at Detroit)

The Pistons have taken over this town from the Red Wings, who play that other winter sport. For years the Red Wings dominated the sports pages of the local newspapers, while the Pistons were mentioned somewhere in agate type on the scoreboard page. Now Gordie Howe and his sons are playing in Houston in another league, the Red Wings are not going well, and suddenly the city has discovered the Pistons.

In fact, both Detroit papers today were filled with stories about the "zone defense" played by teams in the NBA. What provoked the stories was Manny Sokol's decision to call an illegal zone against the Pistons during their game last Sunday against the Capital Bullets. Actually, Manny didn't call an illegal zone per se, instead, he whistled the Pistons for a rare defensive 3-second violation. To wit, if a defensive player is within the sixteen-foot lane and is not within eight feet of *any* opponent he is in violation of the rules. So the referee will quickly call him for a 3-second violation. Or an illegal zone, if you wish.

In one story Ray Scott, the Pistons' coach, argued vociferously that every team in the league plays the zone. In a sense, Scott's right because every team plays the 6-to-8-foot style of defense—but that, according to the rule book, is legal. The referees are quite aware of what is happening, but we go by the rule book. Besides, if every team is playing the zone defense, as Scott insists, then why don't all the coaches shut up about it. Lenny Wirtz and I rehashed the situation during our pre-game meeting and went over the rule book to refamiliarize ourselves with the strict wording of the laws as they applied to zone defenses and defensive 3-second violations. Trouble, we knew, was brewing.

Sure enough, the Pistons got the opening tap, and as they surged down court against the Celtics every player on their bench was on his feet and screaming: "Zone! Zone!

Zone!" *Tweet!* I called time and walked over to the Detroit bench. "Ray," I said to Ray Scott, "you're in big trouble now. I won't put up with any more of this chatter from your bench. You are responsible for the conduct of the personnel on your bench. If I hear any more talk about zones, the technical foul will be on you."

To make sure there was no communication gap between us, I repeated my statement. He nodded his head—and I nodded my head. Then he sat down, and I started to walk back out to the court. Would you believe it? As soon as I turned away, I heard a voice from the Detroit bench say, "Horseshit!" So I said to myself: "Self, you might as well do it right now." So I turned and called a technical foul on Ray Scott. He didn't protest the technical at the time, but as the teams walked off at halftime he stepped up to me and asked if we could have a brief chat. "Sure," I said. "Let me get Tommy Heinsohn over here first." When Heinsohn arrived, Scott asked me why I had called the technical on him.

"It seemed to me that I had to keep control of the game at that time. I can't put up with your anger over something that happened in a previous game."

"What about the technical?" he asked.

"I told you I would not tolerate any more conversation from your bench—and the moment I turned my back there was more conversation," I answered.

"Richie, it wasn't one of my players who yelled at you," Scott said. "It was a spectator."

Unbelievable, but maybe true.

"If the voice was a spectator's, I apologize," I said.

"Don't worry about it," he said.

No matter, the technical served its purpose, and after that brief eruption in the first minute of play both teams settled back and played basketball. Not great basketball, but basketball nonetheless. The Celtics won by 3 points, 85 to 82, but both clubs played poorly throughout. The statisticians couldn't keep track of all the turnovers, and I don't think either team shot 40 percent. The coaches were lost for words after the game.

"We were lucky to survive," Heinsohn said flatly.

Scott laughed. "I hope I get as many chances to get into heaven as the Celtics got in this game," he said.

John Havlicek had an awful game, perhaps the worst game I have ever seen him play. He looked tired and drawn, and said that his shoulder was bothering him. He told me he had spent all day Monday and most of today participating in a Superstars television competition down in Rotonda, Florida, and that every one of his bones ached. Some of the Celtics kidded him about his low finish in the extravaganza, which was won by soccer player Kyle Rote Jr. "Hey, Hondo," someone yelled, "maybe we ought to sign Rote if he's a better athlete than you." Then again, can Young Kyle Rote Jr. dunk a basketball? Or beat Kareem Abdul-Jabbar one-on-one?

Wednesday, February 27 (K.C.-Omaha at Atlanta)

Before leaving Detroit, I called Johnny Nucatola and reported the incident about the zone defenses and Scott's technical foul. I recommended leniency with regard to the $50 fine for technicals in light of what Scott told me about the spectator who might have yelled the expletive. Knowing Ray Scott, I know he wouldn't give me a line of baloney.

Basketball also was the main topic in the Atlanta sports pages as the writers all offered different explanations for the recent suspension of Pistol Pete Maravich by Hawks' Coach Cotton Fitzsimmons. I don't know what Maravich did or did not do to warrant such action, but about the only thing the papers haven't accused him of is hijacking an airliner. What happens between players and management is not any concern of mine, and I could care less about what coaches are getting along with what players and what coaches aren't, but I get the feeling that Pistol Pete will be shooting for some other NBA team next year.

Friday, March 1 (New York at Capital)

There was a message waiting for me when I walked into the dressing room at the Capital Centre about ninety minutes before the start of the Knicks-Bullets game: "Call Johnny *Nocotoller*. Urgent." Poor John. Two officials had called in sick today, and he needed someone to work the Chicago-Golden State game tomorrow night. Could I help him out? "Sure," I said, "I'll fly out to Chicago tomorrow noon." Pause. Long pause. Then, "Richie, the game's in Oakland." Pause. Long pause. Longer pause. Then I said, "Whatever you say, chief." I'm scheduled to work in Portland on Sunday night, so the detour to Oakland won't be that much of a problem, except that I'll have to referee a two-hour basketball game after spending about nine hours in transit from Greenwich to Oakland.

The basketball game played by the Knicks and the Bullets provided a sure sign that the playoffs are near. It was what the players, the coaches, the referees and the spectators, not to mention the golden throats behind the microphones, call a "playoff-type" contest—tight defenses, probing offenses and more strategy sessions than they hold at the Pentagon during an international crisis. It appears that the Knicks and the Bullets will be first-round opponents when the playoffs get underway later this month. Their records are relatively close, and, of course, the team with the best record will have the home-court advantage in the event a seventh game is necessary. So New York rightfully could call tonight's triumph over the Bullets a "big win."

Phil Chenier of the Bullets and Clyde Frazier of the Knicks were alternately brilliant, with Chenier controlling the ball in the first half and Frazier running things in the

(139)

second half as the Knicks rallied to win by 9 points. Frazier *vs.* Chenier may be the best one-on-one matchup in the NBA right now. I look at the way they turn themselves into pretzels with their unbelievable fakes, then I look at my own physique, and feel like a blob of silly putty.

It was a relatively quiet game except for an incident between Elvin Hayes and Bill Bradley. The Big E, who has been a tireless workman for the Bullets during the frequent absences of injured rebounding-specialist Wes Unseld, collided with Bradley as Bill set up a legal pick for one of the Knicks' shooters. Elvin, however, took offense to Bradley's actions, and on the way down the floor he kept talking to Bradley, who seemed to want no part of the action. I was studying them both very carefully. To me, the scene is a part of the mystique of refereeing. I could see that New York probably would be running the same successful play on one of its next trips down the court, with Bradley picking the defense for a clean twenty-foot jump shot by Dave DeBusschere. And I could see Hayes colliding with Bradley again.

And it happened on the very next play. I was sure that Bradley was aware of what would happen, and I knew that Hayes was well aware of what would happen. I knew, too, but I can't prevent such things from happening. The collision was hard, extremely hard. In fact, if Elvin's elbow had been about one inch higher I would have called an "intent-to-injure" foul on him. He didn't move the elbow at all; he just had it up high to begin with—and left it there. Bradley took a good shot—and he staggered backward. I immediately called the foul on Hayes, and Bradley converted the free throw. Elvin did not complain about the foul, of course. Thinking about it, there are times when a referee can say to a player: "Hey, I have an idea what you're going to do, so don't do it." However, we normally don't say it because we only have an *idea.*

Saturday, March 2 (Chicago at Golden State)

I think I employed most of the Great American Traveling Machines today. I drove my own car from Greenwich to Kennedy Airport, caught the 9:00 A.M. jet to San Francisco, helicoptered across the bay to Oakland and then took the jitney to my hotel. I was sound asleep in my hotel room by 1:30 P.M.

Like the Knicks-Bullets game back east last night, this is a *must* contest for both the Chicago Bulls and the Golden State Warriors. The Bulls are trying to track down the Milwaukee Bucks for first place in the Midwest Division, while the Warriors still are battling the Lakers for what probably will be the only playoff berth in the Pacific Division. If Clyde Lee, who has returned to the Golden State line-up after a long siege of assorted injuries, and Nate Thurmond, the man with the bad knees and bad ankles, can remain healthy down the stretch, I think the Warriors will be difficult to beat.

Lee and Thurmond dominated the boards against the Bulls, thus freeing Rick Barry for what he does best—shooting the lights out. I don't think Barry missed more than a couple of shots all night as the Warriors stayed ahead throughout a quiet game. I happened to be standing behind Barry when he released a number of his shots, and I could almost tell the ball would swish through the netting the moment he released it. He has perfect rotation on his jumpers. The ball takes about four turns in reverse, then—boom!—it's dropping through the cords. Barry is indeed a textbook shooter. It's strange. The last time I worked a Golden State game Barry tried to be a playmaker rather than a shooter, and the game before that he wanted to rebound instead of shoot. Tonight he shot—and rarely missed.

And the name of the player who was the lead character in the only incident in an otherwise crisply played game?

Would you believe Jerry Sloan of the Bulls? In the second quarter Sloan went up for a jumper and released the ball cleanly. Thurmond, cutting diagonally across the court, tried to knock the ball away, but he missed it. There was no contact as the ball flew toward the basket. I turned away from Sloan and Thurmond and looked for the continuing action under the boards. However, I managed out of the corner of my eye to catch sight of Nate's legs hitting against Jerry's legs as they both came down onto the floor. Still, the play was long over, and the contact had no effect whatsoever on the shot, which dropped through the basket.

As we started back up court, Sloan was sitting on the floor out of bounds trying to get up. Slowly. In the best Hollywood tradition, he managed to get to his feet. He staggered forward for fifteen or sixteen feet and then proceeded to perform a magnificent pratfall. Give the man an Oscar! I looked over at Sloan evenly, giving him my "What-the-hell-are-you-trying-to-prove?" glare. He looked back at me evenly and said, "—— you!" Naturally I gave him a technical. "You certainly don't think I'm going to let you get away with that, do you?" I said.

Sunday, March 3 (Detroit at Portland)

Look at these statistics. The Trail Blazers took 8 foul shots and made 7, while the Pistons attempted 39 and made 35. So the Pistons won the game by a few dozen points, right? Wrong! They barely squeeked past the Trail Blazers by four points. As some writers asked me after the game, why such a disparity in the free throws? Simple. The Portland offense depends almost entirely upon Geoff Petrie and Sidney Wicks. In fact, Petrie and Wicks accounted for 47 of the 94 shots that Portland took in the game. Both Petrie and Wicks play away from the basket, contentedly shooting twenty-foot jumpers at the expense of everything else. They rarely, if ever, drive for the basket. In this game, for instance, Petrie drove the lane once and Wicks drove twice. Of course, with Bob Lanier standing in the lane looking like the Empire State Building not many players like to drive the middle against the Pistons. And when you don't drive you don't draw many free throws. Petrie scored 32 points, hitting on 15 of 26 from the outside and 2-of-2 from the line, while Wicks scored 24 points, with some 20 of them coming on shots from outside. The Pistons, on the other hand, drove the lane all night and were fouled frequently. "There was an astronomical difference in the free throws," Jack McCloskey, the Portland coach, noted, "but don't blame the referees. They're not the people who were intimidated by Lanier's presence in the middle."

The game was played against a backdrop of two death threats that were phoned to the Portland team's office during the past few days. As a result, the building was swarming with enough security people to guard Fort Knox. Some people tend to pass off death threats as the work of a crank, but I don't think anyone ought to take them lightly. If some character says he's going to kill you, you have to believe him. The league wisely refused to divulge the name of the player who was the subject of the caller's threat. Before the game the players were advised of the increased police protection in the building, but they did not seem to be affected by it. As a matter of fact, one of the security policemen asked me if I wanted to wear a bulletproof vest under my referee's jersey. I had to laugh. "I've got one already," I said. "My thick skin."

Tuesday, March 5 (Detroit at Golden State)

I couldn't believe that the Golden State team I watched tonight against the Pistons was the same Golden State team that had decimated the Chicago Bulls just three nights ago. The Pistons baffled the confused Warriors for 48 minutes, dominating the action at both boards, picking off errant passes at will and stifling the Golden State shooters with solid pressure defense. Nate Thurmond limped around for most of the game, while Clyde Lee could not handle Bob Lanier off the boards. (Who can, for that matter?) And remember those perfect shots Rick Barry kept releasing against the Bulls? In this game it looked as though Rick was shooting a medicine ball instead of a basketball. Somehow he scored 36 points, but he missed about two of every three shots he threw up at the basket—and I don't think he took more than a half dozen high percentage shots all night, that is, close-in, unimpeded shots, like lay-ups. It may sound ridiculous to say that a player had a bad game when he scored 36 points, but I'd say that Rick had a bad game. Worse still for the Warriors, the Lakers were losing to the Trail Blazers in Portland—and the Warriors lost a chance to pick up a game on their blood enemies.

Wednesday, March 6 (Chicago at Houston)

If it's Wednesday, it must be Houston. Everybody should stop off in Houston on their way from San Francisco to New York. I spent the night aboard a jet, then spent the day sightseeing Houston. For me, sightseeing means studying the whiteness of the sheets on the king-sized bed in my hotel room. The Houston Rockets are going nowhere fast, but they still are very dangerous opponents, with strong players such as Rudy Tomjanovich and Calvin Murphy. Chicago, meanwhile, has been on the road for almost two weeks and desperately needs a victory to stay close to Milwaukee in the battle for first place.

Some teams, of course, will try anything to gain a victory, particularly when they need it, so the Bulls applied a bit of courtside psychology to the Rockets before the opening tap. Jim Capers and I had just finished the pre-game meeting with the two captains, Tomjanovich of the Rockets and Chet Walker of the Bulls, and as we walked away Walker suddenly said: "By the way, I want you to watch out for Calvin Murphy tripping people." Tomjanovich, of course, heard Walker's remark, and he immediately repeated it in the Houston huddle around Coach Johnny Egan. Walker's comment seemed to affect Murphy once the game began— in fact, Calvin quickly was called for two offensive fouls.

At the next time out he said to me: "I didn't like what Walker said to you guys before the game. I hope it isn't affecting your calls."

"Not one little bit, Calvin," I said. "You haven't tripped anyone yet, have you?"

"No," he said flatly.

I can't recall ever seeing Murphy tripping other players, but referees must take complaints such as Walker's under advisement. Besides the obvious "psyching" effect of such a remark, there is always the chance that it's true. Late in the game I did call a leg foul on Murphy, but not for tripping. After the game I asked Capers if he had ever seen Calvin trip another player. Jim said he recalled a few Murphy fouls that might have been called tripping, but he couldn't remember Calvin ever tripping another player with deliberate intent. Psychology or not, the Bulls won the game.

On the way to the dressing room Dick Motta was lamenting the long, hard road schedule that the Bulls had just finished. "Sorry, Dick," I said. "You'd better find someone else's shoulder to cry on."

The schedule is something we all must live with. At present I'm nearing the end, thank God, of a stretch during which I will have worked fifteen games in eighteen days. And, unlike the great majority of players in the NBA, the referees work 48 minutes each and every game. Yes, I serve crying towels.

Friday, March 8 (Seattle at Buffalo)

Like Detroit, Buffalo is fast becoming a great basketball town. In their first three years in the NBA, the Braves won, in order, 22, 22 and 21 games, and always finished in last place in their division. Now, unbelievably, they need only two more wins to clinch a playoff position. Eddie Donovan, the shrewd general manager of the Braves who did so much to build the New York Knicks into a championship team several years ago, and Coach Jack Ramsay have built a strong, aggressive team of young players, and I, for one, think the Braves will go a long way in the playoffs.

Bob McAdoo, the big forward from North Carolina, presently leads the NBA in scoring—quite an accomplishment for a kid in just his second season. The P.A. announcer here evokes titters when he exclaims "Two for McAdoo!" every time Bob connects for a basket. Ernie DiGregorio, the rookie guard from Providence, leads the NBA in assists, scores better than 15 points per game and plays defense a lot better than the people who jokingly call him "Ernie-No-D" like to think. Jim McMillian, the sharp-shooting forward Donovan acquired from Los Angeles in the Elmore Smith trade, provides scoring and strong offensive rebounding from one of the corner spots, while Jack Marin, Garfield Heard and Randy Smith also are consistent contributors to the Buffalo attack. In a couple of seasons people will probably be talking about a basketball dynasty in Buffalo. The Braves already draw capacity crowds to the Aud, and the people obviously appreciate the Braves' run-and-gun style because they never leave until after the final whistle.

The Braves were psyched-up for tonight's game against Seattle because they want to make the playoffs through the front door. The place was bedlam from the outset and, not surprisingly, our troubles began very early. With slightly less than four minutes to play in the opening quarter Lee Jones—my officiating partner—called a violation on Ernie

D. for dribbling out of bounds. There was really nothing to argue about because Ernie D. simply dribbled the ball out of bounds.

Buffalo immediately called time out, and Bob Kauffman, the captain of the Braves, who doesn't get to play much anymore, came out to discuss the interpretation of the out-of-bounds dribble with Lee Jones. I was standing at center court, watching them debate the call but otherwise minding my own business for a change. After a while, though, I could see that Lee was having difficulty convincing Kauffman to return to the Buffalo bench, so I moved over toward them.

"I told you that your question involved a referee's judgment—and not a rule—so now go away," Lee was saying to Kauffman as I approached.

Kauffman continued to stand next to Jones, so I said to him: "Bob, you asked a question, you got an answer—and now you're not going to protract this argument, are you? So let's go."

"I didn't get my answer," Kauffman said.

"Yes, you did," I said.

Slowly Kauffman left for the bench, and I turned and walked away. Moments later I heard a buzz run through the crowd, and when I looked around to see what was happening there was Kauffman walking behind Lee Jones and imitating Lee's stiff-legged gait. "You are going way beyond the acceptable proportions," I said to Kauffman. "Mimicking a referee is not among the functions of your job as captain of the Buffalo basketball team. Please return to your bench." As Kauffman and I walked across the court, he suddenly started to circle around me. I had had enough by this time, so I took my whistle and put it in my mouth to signal to Kauffman that the rules were about to land on his head. And he didn't stop. He stood on the court and continued to berate us. *Tweet!* Did that shut him up? Nope. "Bob," I said, "that's one. The second technical is coming instantaneously if you don't shut up and return to your bench." Amazingly, Kauffman continued, so I gave him the second technical and ejected him. It was the first time in my career that I had ever ejected a captain who had not yet been in the game.

Kauffman's ejection seemed to heat the mood of the crowd and the players. Moments later I called an obvious foul on a Buffalo player, and suddenly Rudy Martzke, the publicity director of the Braves, was standing alongside the court, screaming at me. It was not the first time in the game that Martzke had acted like that, but it was going to be the last. I stopped the game, walked over to where he was standing and ordered him to remove himself promptly. To his credit, he left immediately.

Now I was zero-for-two as far as the Buffalo crowd was concerned, and moments later I was zero-for-three when I gave the "safe" sign—meaning no foul—as Spencer Haywood of the SuperSonics blocked one of McAdoo's line-drive jump shots. Haywood turned the shot back with so much force that it seemed as though the ball had been shot from a gun. It was the most forceful block I have ever seen. The Buffalo bench rose up in unison to protest my call. "Keep your seat—or else," I warned Jack Ramsay as I ran back toward the other end of the court.

A smattering of fans began to chant "Powers is a bum! Powers is a bum!" Then the entire crowd began to pick it up when I made what they thought was my fourth straight anti-Buffalo call. It was a simple thing, really. The ball bounced off Randy Smith of the Braves and rolled out of bounds, so I blew my whistle and gave the ball to Seattle. Once again the Buffalo bench rose in unison and began to berate me verbally, while the noise from the crowd was unreal. Listen. The fans have the right and privilege to boo me and call me names. As long as fans don't physically accost an official, they can do anything they want. And no matter what they call me, it's not going to affect me. I have been called a bum in the past and I expect to be called a bum in the future. Show me a referee who hasn't been called a bum, and I'll show you a bad referee.

The anti-Powers sentiments of the crowd and the Buffalo players marred an otherwise superlative basketball game. The teams traded baskets from the opening tap, and near the end of the fourth quarter Jack Marin kept the Braves alive with several key baskets from around the foul line. Buffalo, in fact, led by two points in the closing seconds, but then Jim Fox of Seattle was fouled during some rebounding action under the SuperSonics basket and converted two of his three free throws to send the game into overtime.

Early in the overtime period the Seattle bench complained vigorously that Buffalo was playing an illegal zone defense. I told Bill Russell the same thing I had told Ray Scott a few weeks ago in Detroit: "If the chatter from the bench does not stop, I'll be after you." So it stopped. In fact, when Freddy Brown mumbled something about the alleged zone after he missed an easy shot, Russell yelled out: "Stop complaining. You know how to play against that defense." You know, the way the players in the NBA can shoot, they should be able to defeat any type of defense.

Seattle came on to win the game in overtime. Strangely, we didn't call one foul during the extra session. Still, when the game ended, the Buffalo fans suddenly remembered the name "Powers" and, in unison, told me in no uncertain terms that I had lost the game for the Braves. What really surprised me was that no reporter bothered to come into the dressing room afterwards to ask about the Kauffman ejection and the other plays that had stirred up the crowd in such an anti-Powers rage. So it goes.

Saturday, March 9 (Milwaukee at New York)

I managed to escape from Buffalo unsullied. On the flight to New York I looked over the stat sheet of the Seattle-Buffalo game and noticed that Seattle had been called for 28 personal fouls while Buffalo had been called for 18. Hell, if Seattle had lost the game, I probably would have been accused of being a homer.

I spent most of the day sleeping at home, then drove to Madison Square Garden to work the Knicks-Bucks game. On paper, it should have been a super contest. Actually, it was another blowout, with the Knicks crushing the Bucks and holding them to the unbelievable total of just 72 points. I don't know why, but the Bucks never seem to play very well in the Garden. Maybe it's because the Knicks never let them play well.

Sunday, March 10 (Los Angeles at Boston)

The Celtics have been in a slight slump, probably because John Havlicek has been out of their line-up for several games recuperating from a series of nagging injuries. Anyway, the Lakers almost ran the Celtics off the Boston Garden court during the first quarter of the nationally televised CBS game. In an attempt to stall the Los Angeles attack, the Celtics kept calling time outs. Thank you, Mr. Heinsohn: I needed the time outs almost as badly as the Celtics, because I was working my third game in less than forty hours, and my legs were killing me.

As the Celtics continued to fall behind, Tommy Heinsohn switched his attentions to the referees and started to bait Mark Mano and myself after every call that went against Boston. It seemed to me that Tom was grouching strictly to stimulate his bedraggled team. But we can't let such things get out of hand; so after one exceptionally loud outburst I called a technical foul on Heinsohn and told him to cut out the chatter—or else. Tommy's favorite expression during a basketball game is simple and direct: he raises his hands to ear level and yells "Jesus Christ!" Some night I think I'll tell Heinsohn that on the basketball court I prefer to be called Richie.

Whatever Heinsohn intended with his verbal barrage, it must have worked. Havlicek regained his sharp edge as play progressed, the Celtics rallied from a tremendous deficit and shattered the Lakers in the final quarter, winning by more than 10 points. It was, as the players like to say, a "good victory" for Boston and a "bad loss" for Los Angeles. At the airport I met Pat Summerall, the CBS play-by-play man, and Bill MacPhail, the head of the sports division at CBS-TV. They asked me why Heinsohn and I hadn't looked at each other while I was giving Tommy his technical.

"What makes you ask that question?" I said.

"We had a camera on the two of you," Summerall said, "and the way you two guys ignored each other was so unusual that we showed it on instant replay a couple of times."

"I don't know why we didn't look at one another," I said. "It just happened that way."

Cripes! Am I supposed to look at people when the cameras are focused on me? Are they supposed to look at me? Maybe I ought to take a correspondence course in the fine art of acting.

Tuesday, March 12 (Atlanta at Cleveland)

At halftime my partner, Mark Mano, mentioned that some Buffalo writer had written a defamatory article about me in Sunday's edition of the Buffalo *Courier-Express*. I told Mano I hadn't read the story because I rarely read news accounts of games I had worked. After the game I found a restaurant that was open in downtown Cleveland, had a bite to eat and a couple of Double Ds, went to my room and was greeted by a ringing telephone. It was Mano. Someone had dropped by his hotel room and slipped the article from the Buffalo paper under his door. He wanted to read it to me. "Are you sitting down, Richie?" he asked.

I started to listen, but after less than a half minute I put the phone down on the bed by my side—and for the next several minutes all I could hear was his mumbling. Why was he doing this to me? He couldn't be that interested in what the Buffalo paper had to say, and if he was that interested, he should have left the story under my door. When he finished he asked: "What do you think of that?" I said, "Who cares? That's one man's opinion."

Needless to say, I had difficulty getting to sleep after Mano's phone call. Press comments normally don't bother me, but there was something about the tone of this Buffalo story that smacked of revenge. I don't know, really, because I have not read the entire story. I do know that I will call Nick Curran, the director of public relations for the NBA, in New York tomorrow morning and ask him to get me a clip of the story so that I can read it first hand. Until then I don't want to comment on hearsay.

In the past I've had some run-ins with many of the most distinguished sports journalists in the country. And as those members of the fourth estate came to learn, Richie Powers is a stand-up guy. I don't back off from criticism or praise. And I speak my mind. For instance, back in the 1960s Earl Strom and I were working the seventh game of the great Boston-Philadelphia series when the Celtics squeeked out a victory despite the famous "wire" incident involving Bill Russell. With 15 seconds to play in the game, Boston had a 1-point lead and Russell was trying to toss the ball in-bounds from underneath the basket that the Celtics were defending. At the count of three, two seconds before Boston would have lost the ball, Russell passed the ball to a Celtic teammate but it struck the guide-wire support for the basket en route. Strom whistled the play dead and gave the ball to Philadelphia, which now had a chance to win the game and the series. There were only a handful of seconds left when Earl handed the ball to Hal Greer underneath the basket, who was standing in practically the same spot that Russell had stood only moments before.

According to the play that Philadelphia had worked out, Chet Walker was supposed to run in, give a fake, take the ball on the in-bounds pass and then throw up a jumper. Well, when Greer got the ball, I was standing next to Walker and staring into the eyes of John Havlicek, who was covering Walker very closely. Greer passed the ball toward Walker, but Havlicek could tell from Walker's reaction that the pass-in was short. So Havlicek jumped up, threw out his left arm and the ball hit it. At that moment I signaled for the clock to begin, and in the next instant Sam Jones of the Celtics stormed in, scooped up the ball and proceeded to kill the clock. Havlicek had made one of the great clutch plays in the history of professional basketball, and the Celtics had been saved. There was no argument whatsoever from any player on the Philadelphia team, either.

Well, the next morning I picked up the *New York Daily News* and came across Dick Young's column. Alongside Young's story was a little cartoon of a referee in action. Young obviously did not appreciate the job that Earl and I had done the night before in Boston, because he wrote that if Mendy Rudolph and Sid Borgia had worked the game, Philadelphia would have won because they would have called the foul where Walker was "belted" by Havlicek at the end of the game. I had never met Young. I also suspected that he probably saw the game on TV. I was there, the referee involved in the play, and miles away he wrote that I had no integrity and no guts. Listen. There was no foul on the play. The Celtics knew it, the Philadelphia team knew it.

So I picked up a pen and wrote a letter to Mr. Young. I never received an answer from him, but in another column about a month later, Young wrote this message: "Dear Richie. How can you explain Philadelphia beating New York by 10 points in Philadelphia one night, and New York beating Philadelphia by 10 points the next night in New York?" I wrote back to Mr. Young and asked him what the hell business was it of mine to know why Philadelphia beat

New York one night and New York beat Philadelphia the next.

They were not my first run-ins with Mr. Young. In my second year as an NBA referee I was working the first game of a double-header at the Garden between the St. Louis Hawks and the Fort Wayne Pistons. According to the writers in those days—and, in fact, according to the writers today—the referees went out of their way to protect the superstars from fouling out. Late in this game I called a foul on Bob Pettit of the Hawks. It was Pettit's sixth foul, so he had to leave the game. As it was, he left without argument. He grimaced, but it was not one of those haunting Bob Boozer grimaces. So, as I walked back up court, a reporter yelled at me: "Horseshit foul, Powers!" I turned around, looked for a moment—and there was Dick Young going full blast. What consummate gall! The day before, Young had written that referees protect superstars, and now here's one of the top superstars in the game fouling out on an infraction that is in his opinion "horseshit." Amazing!

Wednesday, March 13 (Los Angeles at Philadelphia)

I spoke to Nick Curran this morning and he said that he would send the Buffalo article to me by special delivery. We get the mail between 9:30 and 10:00 A.M. in Greenwich, so the story ought to make for some interesting reading tomorrow over morning coffee. Today it was a routine trip to Philadelphia, routine meaning chaos. Instead of arriving in Philadelphia at midday, I did not land at the airport until almost 7:00 P.M., thanks to a faulty oil regulator on the plane that caused interminable delays. Of course, that was semipredictable because nothing ever goes right when I travel to Philadelphia.

The Lakers murdered the 76ers in a body-bender as Gail Goodrich threw in 38 points. The game was so rough that on one in-bounds play I gave the ball to a Philadelphia player and yelled: "First and ten!"

As we walked off the court at the end, Fred Carter of the 76ers told me that I owe his team two fast breaks next season. I guess I do, too. With 20 seconds to play in the first half, the Lakers had the ball and moved it around for one last shot. They missed the shot, Philadelphia rebounded and then I heard this whistle blowing as the 76ers were racing down court. Naturally I looked around to see who had blown it. Paul Mihalak, my partner, professed innocence. So who blew the whistle? Me! I couldn't believe it. Carter asked me why I blew the whistle. "Freddy, I don't have the faintest idea," I said. I can't remember the last time I did such a thing, but I'm sure that it happened in Philadelphia and I'm also sure that the next such whistle also will happen in Philadelphia. Once I recovered my composure, I gave the ball to the 76ers, but they didn't have time to score.

Shortly after the intermission, the 76ers lost another fast-break possibility when Mihalak's whistle failed to work as he called a walking violation on Elmore Smith. Not hearing any whistle, the 76ers stole the ball from Smith, raced down court and were headed for an easy basket when I interrupted them with my whistle. The 4 points Philadelphia probably would have scored on the fast breaks fortunately were not a factor in the game.

I had at least one good laugh toward the end, though, when Mihalak, probably the best young official in the league, gave me a good-natured twitting. I blew my whistle for a foul on the Lakers, but as it turned out Paul beat my whistle by a fraction of a second. No problem, it happens all the time. So what does Paul do next? He says to me: "Good call, Richie." Why that smart-assed young kid! It took me seventeen years to act that way, and here's Mihalak doing it already. Doesn't he have any respect for age and experience?

Thursday, March 14 (Off-day)

I now have in my possession the story written by the columnist in Buffalo whose name turns out to be Phil Ranallo. It is the most villifying thing I have ever read about anyone—and in my view a super cheap shot. So cheap that his remarks don't deserve to make these pages. After reading it, I called Nick Curran and asked him who Phil Ranallo was. Nick told me that four years ago I had asked the Buffalo P.R. director and a man sitting alongside him at the press table to control their comments during a game. It seems that the man sitting next to the P.R. guy was Phil Ranallo. Well, it sure took him a long time to come into the open with his thoughts about Powers.

Friday, March 15 (Buffalo at Chicago)

My record as a prognosticator compares favorably with Garo Yepremian's record as a foreward passer, but I was right for once tonight when I told Jim Capers before the game that the Chicago Bulls would probably chase the Braves back to Buffalo by the end of the first quarter. The Buffalo players played as if their minds were a thousand miles away, while the Chicago players operated with the enthusiasm and vigor of ten rookies trying to make the varsity. The situation was predictable. Buffalo had clinched a playoff berth several nights ago, earning the right to meet the Boston Celtics in the first round. And the Buffalo players had also spent the previous two days celebrating their accomplishment. Chicago, on the other hand, is still locked in a race for good playoff position. The Bulls must win as many games as they can in order to secure home-court advantage for the "if necessary" seventh game in the first round. As I expected, the Bulls routed the Braves.

Sunday, March 17 (Houston at K.C.–Omaha)

I flew home late Friday, and flew here yesterday for this afternoon's game between the Kings and the Houston Rockets. My legs are starting to bother me again. The muscles are sore and stiff, and it takes me almost the entire first quarter to get them working properly. I think I'll start going to athletic clubs when I'm on the road and try to jog a few miles on their indoor tracks. As a rule, we cannot warm up properly before a game because of the cramped conditions of the dressing rooms in the NBA. We can't exercise in the rooms, and we can't go running up and down the corridors. I used to run in place for five or six minutes before a game, but that never accomplished much.

As always, the Houston team was very noisy, particularly when it fell behind by 23 points to Kansas City–Omaha in the early going before rallying to lose by a respectable six or seven points. On one routine foul Cliff Meely of the Rockets called Hugh Evans, my officiating partner, a "blind" magic word, so we gave Meely a technical almost simultaneously. Only one technical counted, of course, but then Meely added insult to injury by looking at me and calling me a "blind" magic word, too. He kept repeating this opinion long after I had ejected him via the two-technicals route. Meely really should have been given about seven technicals. I hope he got his jollies.

Later Evans called a technical on Sam Lacey of the Kings. Just before the technical, Lacey had said something to me to the effect that he just couldn't get going in the game. Well, after the technical he played super, getting all the rebounds and scoring a batch of baskets. And then, with the Kings pulling away to a big lead thanks to Lacey's strong play, he said to Evans: "Thanks for the technical. I needed that."

Wednesday, March 20 (Milwaukee at Los Angeles)

Facing a win-or-else predicament, the Lakers responded to the pressure with a convincing rout of the Milwaukee Bucks at the frantic Forum in Inglewood. Last week Los Angeles lost twice to Golden State, and it appeared that the Lakers were dead for the first time in Jerry West's career. But the Bucks helped the Lakers by beating the Warriors last night in Oakland, and tonight the Warriors lost in Seattle while the Lakers were winning at home in Los Angeles—so suddenly the Lakers aren't so dead anymore. In fact, the Lakers now lead the Warriors by several percentage points.

Los Angeles was hyperactive from the start, with Elmore Smith controlling the boards, blocking out Kareem Abdul-Jabbar very effectively. Paul Mihalak and I had to call a bunch of technical fouls to keep things in order, but we did our job. Paul hit Hubie Brown, the assistant coach of the Bucks, while I gave technicals to Elmore Smith (for throwing the ball into the stands in disgust), the Milwaukee team (for playing a terribly disguised illegal zone that even a four-year-old could have spotted) and finally to Bucks Coach Larry Costello. Larry was obviously frustrated by the inability of his team to handle the Lakers, and when the Lakers continued to pile it on in the final quarter he just couldn't take it anymore. I was under the basket, and when the play cleared I saw Costello standing in front of the bench. Not the Milwaukee bench, mind you. The Los Angeles bench.

I stopped the game and called the technical, which Costello accepted without one word of protest. Moments later, though, he started to walk out onto the court toward Paul Mihalak. So I called Technical No. 2. Costello seemed to be in a fog, so I tapped him on the shoulder and said, "Larry, you've had two—and you're ejected." Costello turned toward me and said: "Yeah, Richie, I'll be with you in just a moment." Cripes, I felt as though I had just told him that his laundry was done. Then Larry turned and walked calmly back to the Bucks bench, picked up his clipboard and departed the premises. It was one of the strangest ejections I have ever been involved in.

By the way, the next time I see Ed Batogowski I'll have to apologize to him for that lecture I gave him on the proper ball-tossing technique on tap plays. At the start of the second half tonight I was standing between Mr. Jabbar and Mr. Smith, staring them in the kneecaps, and when I tossed the ball up, they both leaped up, too. As Smith vaulted into the air, his leg snapped out and kicked me in the groin. It was the first time all year that I had been hit on a tap play and, God, was I in pain. I stopped the game to get a breather, and Dr. Bob Kerlan, the famed specialist who has treated most of the great athletes in the world, came over to examine me. Some of the players kidded me about the injury, but goddammit it was no laughing matter. In fact it still hurts like hell although a few Double Ds ought to soothe the pain. I'm just glad that tomorrow is an off-day.

Thursday, March 21 (Off-day)

I called Johnny Nucatola at 7:00 A.M. Los Angeles time, which meant 10:00 A.M. back in New York, and gave him my report on the Lakers-Bucks game. I also suggested that he make a switch in the refereeing assignments for tomorrow night's games. The Los Angeles papers are all excited about the Lakers surge toward a playoff berth, and the tone of all the advance stories for Friday night's game against Chicago is that the "Bullies from the Windy City are coming into the city of the angels to play our saints—the Lakers." So I told John maybe he should keep me in Los Angeles to work the Chicago-Lakers game with Mendy Rudolph, and send Rudolph's partner—Jim Capers—over to Phoenix to work the Braves-Suns game that will have no direct bearing on the final standings or the playoffs. Nucatola agreed and said he would inform the other officials of the change in plans.

Hold it, now. I know that I said a while back that there are no "big" games for the referees. True. However, the Chicago–Los Angeles game tomorrow night is a "big" game for both clubs and may provide considerable fireworks. Jim Capers is one of the most talented young referees in the game, and I'm sure that he would handle the Bulls-Lakers contest without any complications. However, I think the NBA ought to protect itself when such games suddenly pop up by using the most experienced referees available. In this case, Nucatola happens to have the No. 1 and No. 2 officials on the seniority list—Mendy Rudolph and Richie Powers, respectively—here on the Coast, and he can use us without causing hardship elsewhere.

Knowing Jim Capers, I don't believe he will be too upset with the change of assignment. Last-minute switches don't occur too often in the modern-day NBA, but in the old days the various chiefs-of-referees never hesitated to change referees at the last minute for reasons that were either stupid or absurd, or both. Some years ago, for instance, I was working a semifinal playoff series involving the Minneapolis Lakers and the St. Louis Hawks. I was scheduled to work the seventh and final game, but shortly before the tap-off I received a call from Jocko Collins, the supervisor in those days. "St. Louis wants a more experienced referee," Jocko told me, "so we're taking you out of the game for your own protection." That made sense. However, I found out the next day that the real reason I was removed from the game was that Minneapolis had won the three playoff games I had worked in the series and the St. Louis management felt that I either favored the Lakers or was their good-luck charm. I had the last laugh, though, because even without Powers working his voodoo against them, the Hawks still lost the seventh game to the Lakers.

What really got me about the incident was that in the old

days we worked on a pay-by-game situation. No work, no pay. Not surprisingly, the pay-by-game rule created some ill feelings among the officials, particularly the older officials who hated it when a young squirt like Richie Powers would come along and get a few extra jobs in the playoffs. And I hated it when a young squirt like Richie Powers didn't get extra jobs in the playoffs. In many ways this is still a problem for the league office. Right now, in fact, I know that Johnny Nucatola and Walter Kennedy are evaluating the officials prior to selecting the eight referees who will work regularly in the playoffs. I suspect that, as always, they will decide to use the more experienced officials on the staff. The kids will be miffed, and some of them will resent the older officials, but such feelings are only natural. The kids work all season, then get bumped from the playoffs— and, well, why shouldn't they be angry. It costs them money.

For the playoffs, I will be paid $550 per game in the quarter finals, $650 per game in the semifinals and $800 per game in the finals. Realistically, I expect to make about $7,500.

Friday, March 22 (Chicago at Los Angeles)

Now I don't know what to think. Like most people in Los Angeles, I thought the Bulls-Lakers game would be a mini-war, with a lot of fighting, verbalizing and overaggressive ball hawking, not to mention a slew of technical fouls. I expected a football game. However, much to my surprise what we had instead was one of the quietest games I have ever refereed. The players were on their best behavior, the coaches didn't say anything except hello and goodbye, and we didn't make even one controversial decision all night as the Lakers won a close struggle.

Back at the hotel lounge I encountered a spirited group of Lakers fans who were celebrating the victory—or, rather, overcelebrating the victory. One man in particular kept bothering me, telling me that I was a horseshit referee, that my family's tree was a weeping willow, that I was too short and too fat and too goddamned noisy and opinionated to be any good at all. Then, in the next breath, this character said to me: "Hey, do me a favor, willya? Willya say hello to Jack Twyman for me the next time you see him."

Jack Twyman. A great man, really, and not just a great basketball player during his years with the Cincinnati Royals. Twyman became the late Maurice Stokes' legal guardian when Stokes contracted a rare form of meningitis and had to spend the remaining years of his life institutionalized in a wheel chair. I know that Twyman spent countless hours of his own time working to accumulate funds to pay Stokes' hospital costs. Jack was a gentlemen during his career, too, but one night here in Los Angeles he lost his cool for maybe the only time in his career.

He was mad about something, and suddenly in the middle of the game he told me what I could do with myself in no uncertain terms. I gave him a technical foul and ejected him from the game. Instead of going to the dressing room in accordance with the rules, Twyman continued to sit on the Royals bench. Finally I looked at Twyman and said: "Jack, you'd better get your ass off the bench." So he left for the dressing room. Well, Charlie Wolf, the Cincinnati coach, took great exception to my use of the word "ass" and ripped me from stem-to-stern for using such gross profanity on the court.

I had forgotten about the incident until I received a letter from Maurice Podoloff, then the president of the NBA, in which he quoted from a letter he had received from a real estate man in Los Angeles who was shocked by my use of the word "ass" in my conversation with Mr. Twyman. The real estate man said that I was a disgrace to the game. Maybe "ass" was an inopportune choice of words, but what Twyman said to me was both polysyllabic and hyphenated —and not found in any dictionary. So I took my pen and wrote to the real estate man, telling him exactly what Twyman had said. I also told him that I could have told Twyman to take his bottom, his rear, his can or even his gluteus maximus to the dressing room, but that I had chosen a word that each of us uses regularly.

Except Charlie Wolf, that is. In the end I had to laugh.

Saturday, March 23 (off-day)

I called Paul Mihalak when I arrived in Seattle and asked him how the game had gone in Phoenix last night. "We had big trouble," Paul said. "Big trouble." Cripes, I switched assignments to handle a game where big trouble was expected, so the big trouble happened in the game I was supposed to work in the first place. Mihalak said that Rick Roberson of Portland had slugged Neal Walk of Phoenix and that the ensuing battle was better than a lot of heavyweight championship fights. But the bizarre thing about the game was that Portland had to play a rarely used benchwarmer named LaRue Martin in the final moments because of foul problems, and then Martin won the game by hitting two jump shots and a couple of free throws.

It reminded me of an old Charlie Eckman story when Eckman, a referee who went straight and became an NBA coach, handled the Fort Wayne Zollner Pistons. Eckman's best player was Larry Foust, a center who stood about 6 feet 10 inches and weighed around 280 pounds. In a game at Minneapolis, Foust was suffering from an intestinal virus and kept running to the dressing room every ten minutes to visit the toilet. Late in the game Foust, who had scored more than 30 points for the Pistons to singlehandedly keep them in the game, suddenly became ill again and ran off to the dressing room. Eckman signaled for Bob Houbregs to replace Foust until Larry returned from the treatment room. In rapid order, Houbregs threw in a twenty-five-foot hook shot to bring the Pistons to within 1 point of the

Lakers with 20 seconds to play in the game, then he threw in a thirty-five-foot hook shot to win the game for the Pistons at the buzzer. Eckman sat in stunned disbelief on the bench. After the game he laughed and said, "My coaching genius tonight was based on the fact that my best player had to go to the bathroom."

Sunday, March 24 (Chicago at Seattle)

Bill Russell made Paul and me laugh in the final moments of the game, and I suspect that Russell was laughing himself, even though his SuperSonics were losing the game. One of the Seattle centers was in foul trouble, so Russell removed him from the game and inserted Vester Marshall to play center against Tom Boerwinkle of the Bulls. Boerwinkle stands 6 feet 11 inches and weighs a solid 280 pounds, while Marshall is a slim 6 feet 9 inches and 220 pounds. "Don't let Boerwinkle push you around, now," Russell commanded Marshall. Russell never says anything softly, so his orders were heard by the Seattle players, some nearby fans, the people at the press table and the referees —and suddenly everyone was laughing. "That's easy for you to say," I mentioned to Russell. "Sending Marshall against Boerwinkle is like going after an elephant with a popgun.

Tuesday, March 26 (Portland at Golden State)

Golden State beat Portland as Rick Barry scored 64 points, but the Warriors were eliminated from playoff contention because the Lakers beat the SuperSonics in Los Angeles. When Barry left the game in the closing minutes, I gave him the basketball—his 64 points were some kind of record—and he threw it into the stands. For a moment I thought he was throwing it to the fans, but his wife Pam caught it with a neat two-handed, over-the-head grab. Barry's hot shooting was in sharp contrast to the dismal shooting of Portland's Sidney Wicks, who hit only 4 of the 18 shots he threw up during the first half.

At the start of the second half, Wicks told me that the Portland team wanted us to use a new basketball. I was tempted to tell Mr. Wicks that Mr. Barry did not think there was anything wrong with the basketball we had used in the first half, but for once I smartly kept my lip zipped. In the old days we used to get three basketballs before each game, and then we'd inflate them and test them for proper bounce and feel. All three balls were interchanged during the game. One night years ago Bob Pettit of the St. Louis Hawks was standing at the foul line when he suddenly threw the basketball to the ballboy and received a new one in return.

"What's the matter, Bob?" I asked.

"I didn't like that other ball," he said.

"Bob, you don't have that privilege," I said.

I retrieved the ball Pettit had tossed to the ballboy, gave it to him and told him to shoot it. We finished the game under those conditions, but later that night Pettit and I had a heated discussion about the subject. "Listen, Bob," I said, ending the debate, "if every player in the game wanted to play with his own ball, we'd have ten different balls and utter chaos. I'm the arbiter, and you'll play with the ball I give you."

Right now I have a heavy pain in my chest. It feels as though a half a grape has developed in the middle of my chest. So I called the doctor to our dressing room and he gave me a quick examination. He thinks I may have a bone tumor, and he wants me to go home immediately and have the chest X-rayed. Whew! I'm glad it wasn't a heart condition. Still, I was pretty nervous about the growth, so after the game I forgot about my usual Double Ds and had a Fresca. Two Frescas, in fact. Then I fell asleep.

Wednesday, March 27 (Golden State at Portland)

I was going to call Johnny Nucatola and suggest that he find another referee to work the Warriors–Trail Blazers rematch, but what the hell. It's the last game of the regular season, and one more NBA game is not going to kill me. I feel a little better, but I still think I've got something like a toothache in the middle of my chest.

It was another rainy night in Portland. The Golden State players were understandably depressed by their failure to make the playoffs, but the Portland players and the Portland fans, all ten thousand of them attending the meaningless game, were bounding with joy because the Trail Blazers have just scored their most important victory of the season—beating the Philadelphia 76ers in the traditional coin toss to determine which team gets the No. 1 pick in the annual draft of college talent. The Trail Blazers already have indicated that they will use that No. 1 pick to select Bill Walton, the 6-foot 10-inch All-Everything from UCLA. If the Trail Blazers sign Walton, and I understand that negotiations are already proceeding in that direction, they no doubt will become instant contenders for the Pacific Division championship. And if that happens, they'll have to build an addition onto the Portland Memorial Coliseum to hold the fanatics.

The Trail Blazers won the final game, and so the season has ended. I traveled some 135,000 miles to work 90 games, the heaviest schedule in my career. I ejected about a dozen players and about a half-dozen coaches, and once again I won the Golden T award for calling the most technical fouls.

The season started on an injury note as I wondered about the condition of my legs, and now it ends on an injury note as I'm wondering what's wrong with my chest. Maybe it's all in my head. I can't say I'm overjoyed that the season is over because Richie Powers will be technically unemployed at the conclusion of the playoffs. We work from season-to-season in the NBA, and who knows? Maybe I won't be rehired next year.

Thursday, March 28 (Off-day)

As Dave DeBusschere likes to say, the "second season" is here. It's playoff time in the NBA, the dawning of that annual rite of spring as the eight best teams over the 82-game regular season schedule now begin competition for the NBA Championship. The "second season" lasts a minimum of 4 games and a maximum of 21, depending, of course, how each team handles the do-or-die pressure that so distinguishes the playoffs from the regular schedule. On paper, it seems to me that only the Milwaukee–Los Angeles quarter-final-round series may end quickly; indeed, the Bucks, even without the injured Lucius Allen in the backcourt, have too much power, too much strength and too much Jabbar for the injury-riddled Lakers. The New York–Capital match-up pits two defense-minded teams, while the Detroit-Chicago confrontation pits the most physical clubs in the sport. Not many people give Buffalo much of a chance against the Boston Celtics, but the young Braves have acquired a definite winning attitude and don't seem scared at all by the thought of competing in the playoffs for the first time.

For the playoffs, Commissioner Walter Kennedy, Supervisor-of-Officials Johnny Nucatola and Referee-in-Chief Mendy Rudolph have decided to employ steady teams of referees—at least at the start. This is a great departure from the NBA's standard operating procedure during the regular season, when we work with a different official practically every game. I know they weighed every imaginable factor before coming up with the four officiating teams for the start of the second season, too. Age, personalities, temperament, life-style and ability. Finding the perfect blend was not an easy job.

I will be working with Jake O'Donnell. Oddly, Jake and I did not work together in even one game during the regular season. And I worry about how well we'll work together during these playoffs. I'm an outsider with regards to the referees' association, and Jake, of course, is the president of the group. We have crossed swords on these political matters in the past, and I expect that we will cross swords again in the future. For these reasons there may be great tensions between us, but we cannot let them affect our performance.

Friday, March 29 (Capital at New York)

I'm really smart. I drove down to the gas station yesterday, had the snow tires removed from my car, and woke up this morning to discover eight inches of snow on the ground. After my morning coffee, I drove to the hospital to see Dr. Bill Deegan about my chest. He took several X-rays, then told me there is a tumor on the sixth rib that is breaking through the joint between the rib and the sternum. Dr. Deegan consulted with a Dr. Nickerson, and they both agreed that the growth could be cut out but that it probably would grow back. They want me to leave things as they are for now and report back for another examination when the season is over in six weeks.

The roads were still in treacherous condition in late afternoon, so I left my car at home and rode the Penn Central local from Greenwich to New York, with stops in Port Chester, Rye, Harrison, Mamaroneck, Larchmont, New Rochelle, Pelham, Mount Vernon and 125th Street, and then hopped a cab across town to the Garden. When I walked through the doors at the employees' entrance on the corner of 33rd Street and Eighth Avenue, I could smell the playoff atmosphere. True. The circus always plays the Garden at the time of the basketball playoffs, and the building reeks with the aroma of sawdust, perspiration and elephant dung.

I shook hands with Jake O'Donnell in the dressing room, but we didn't have much to say to each other. We both were very conscious of the situation, and neither of us obviously wanted to force the issue. Knowing the tensions that existed between us, Johnny Nucatola came into the room before the start of the Knicks-Bullets game and wished us good luck. Actually, he just wanted to calm us down. When Nucatola left, I told Jake that we had to maintain control of the game and of ourselves at the expense of everything else. I also reminded him that we had to remain in visual contact at all times, and that we should cool it whenever both of us happened to blow our whistles at the same time. In other words, we had to communicate, not play dictator.

The Bullets ran away from the Knicks at the start, with Elvin Hayes dominating both boards and scoring from everywhere on the court. Jake and I worked together beautifully, and, in fact, we had a meeting of the minds on every call during the first quarter. For the most part we had a quiet time, but then late in the second quarter Kevin Porter of the Bullets complained to me that Willis Reed of the Knicks had held him on a pick play.

Actually, Porter had held Reed on the play, and Reed, seeing Porter trying to win the sympathy vote of an official, came over and began to complain bitterly about Porter's actions. I listened and listened and listened, and I repeatedly told Reed to stop the conversaton because I had heard enough. However, Reed refused to end his verbal tirade, even after I had warned him for the fourth time that I had heard more than enough. Finally, I said to myself: "What the hell is this? It's no different from a regular game." So I gave Reed a technical foul. As I did, I announced loud enough for everyone to hear: "This game is no different!" The players all got my message, and the debating society took a break.

Back in the dressing room at halftime Jake and I were stretched out, relaxing our legs and settling our minds, when the door suddenly opened and Nucatola walked in. Cripes, what the hell had we done wrong now? Nucatola *never* comes into the referees' dressing room at halftime unless there has been a crisis of some sort. "I want you men to know," he said, "that you just worked the greatest half of officiating that I have ever seen." Jake and I were stunned—and speechless. Nucatola said he had to come and see us because everything we had called in that first half was absolutely correct. And then he turned around and walked out.

I don't believe we missed any calls of any sort in the second half, either, as the Knicks rallied behind Bill Bradley's hot shooting hand and beat the Bullets to take a 1–0 lead in the best-of-seven series. It had to be a galling defeat for Hayes, who scored more than 40 points and picked off more than 20 rebounds in one of the most dominating exhibitions of basketball I have ever seen. On the other hand, it was a great night for the referees. I told Jake afterwards that he worked as fine a game as any partner I have ever had in the NBA. I meant it, too.

Saturday, March 30 (Buffalo at Boston)

Dave Cowens of the Celtics did a heavy number tonight on (1) Richie Powers and (2) the Buffalo Braves. In the early minutes of the Boston-Buffalo series opener I had to handle a jump ball between Cowens and Bob McAdoo. Cowens was on my left, McAdoo was on my right, and I had to step in very quickly and get the ball up very quickly—or else one of them might beat the toss. In my haste to throw the ball up quickly and accurately, I somehow managed to get stuck between Cowens and McAdoo as they were leaping for the ball. Cowens accidentally caught me with a Joe Palooka-ish right hand to the solar plexus, just below my bad rib. For a moment I thought the lights were going out. Frank Challant, the Boston trainer who had helped treat my injured thigh in last season's playoffs, rushed over to see if my leg was hurting again, and I think I even asked him for the smelling salts. I delayed the game for a few more minutes, but I still was feeling a twinge of pain when play resumed. For a brief time I thought that I should have Paul Mihalak, the alternate official for the game, take my place temporarily on the court, but I managed to run off the pain, if not the headache. If Cowens wants to become a contender for the heavyweight title, I'll be glad to become one of his backers.

What Cowens did to me, though, was nothing compared to what he did to the Braves. Buffalo bombed Boston throughout the first three quarters, piling up a lead of more than 20 points. Playoff pressure? The Braves were laughing at it. As Cowens and McAdoo lined up for the tap-off to begin the fourth quarter, I moved between them with some uneasiness. After Cowens had accidentally hit me on that early jump ball, I told Jake O'Donnell that I wanted to make all the tosses during the remainder of the game. Why? Mental reasons. I was afraid that if I backed away from tosses in this game that I might never be able to make them again. The tap-off for the final quarter went smoothly, however, as Cowens batted the ball to one of the Celtics and headed for the basket. He ran into one of the Braves en route, though, and was given his fourth personal foul of the game. Seconds later he picked up his fifth foul when he crashed into McAdoo while attempting to block a shot. Cowens now was one foul short of the limit, one short of ejection, and by all rights the Celtics should have been dead.

Instead, for the final 11 minutes of the game it was one man against five: Cowens against the Braves. When Buffalo decided to attack Cowens' position in an attempt to foul him out of the game, Cowens decided that he should attack the Braves. And he did. He stole balls. He blocked shots.

He owned *both* boards. He intimidated shooters. He scored on sweeping hooks from in close, lefty jumpers from out deep, and brilliant drives down the lane. Cowens scored 22 points in those 11 minutes, and the proud Celtics, responding to his charge, outscored the Braves 39 to 16 to turn a certain defeat into an incredible triumph. The Braves could not halt the steamroller, and they were understandably depressed when they left the Boston Garden.

Except for Cowens' late pyrotechnics, it was a quiet game. Strangely quiet, because Jack Ramsay and Tommy Heinsohn normally are two of the better referee-baiters in the NBA. In this game their conduct was exemplary. Sure, Jake and I gave them an occasional warning, but we never had any real problems with the coaches. Better yet, Jake and I once again had a great rapport throughout the game. We didn't miss a call, as far as I could tell.

Sunday, March 31 (Off-day)

Before watching the Bullets beat the Knicks in the CBS-TV game, I called Johnny Nucatola and told him that I thought the Powers-O'Donnell team was working very well so far. Jake and I seem to be reaching a meeting of the minds without doing too much talking about it, accepting each other, and forgetting the trivial politics. Hell, I had thought that the NBA would have to bring in Dr. Kissinger to settle some of our disputes.

Monday, April 1 (Chicago at Detroit)

Judging from newspaper accounts here, the Pistons and the Bulls had something more than a basketball game yesterday in Chicago. One Detroit paper accused the Bulls of playing dirty basketball and another paper went on to claim the Bulls played dirty football. I'm sure the Chicago papers said the same things about the Pistons, who happened to upset the Bulls in that opening game. Personally, I don't agree with any of this talk of "dirty" basketball teams. Both the Bulls and the Pistons are well-coached teams that know their limitations and constantly work to keep their mistakes to a minimum. The only problem the Pistons and the Bulls cause me is that they seem to be involved in more away-from-the-ball incidents than most teams in the NBA.

Jake and I must keep close tabs on Jerry Sloan and Norm Van Lier of the Bulls. We've got to know what they're doing every moment they are on the court, otherwise they'll take advantage of us. They'll flop or tumble or attempt anything to make it seem as though they were fouled. If we don't see what they're doing, they might just get away with something. It's called "Beat the Referee." Some people might call it cheating, but it's not. It's part of the game, and the referees learn to accept it.

As a general rule, the tempo of a game is set during the first four or five minutes of play. In tonight's game, the first five fouls came quickly, as I had expected, and they all happened to be away-from-the-ball fouls, as I had expected. Jake and I handled the fouls very well, and without incident. Then, late in the quarter Dick Motta, the Chicago coach, said to Jake: "I see you've been reading the papers." What Dick meant was he thought Jake was calling fouls very closely on the Bulls because of the strong anti-Chicago remarks in the local papers. Jake responded to Motta's crack by walking over to the Chicago bench and waving his finger in Dick's face, warning him that such conduct would not be tolerated any longer. Motta zipped his lip, and at the half he told Jake that he had not meant anything personal by the remark. O'Donnell nodded his head, indicating case closed. Then Motta said, "Jake, I also know that referee's can't read." Jake and I couldn't help laughing.

Despite his one-liners, Motta was a desperate coach after Sunday's loss at home, and the Bulls responded with a 108 to 103 victory over the Pistons to even the series at one game apiece. Believe it or not, it was Chicago's first playoff victory on the road after eighteen straight losses over the last nine years.

And Ol' Double D is two-for-two in the injury department. Anytime a 5-foot 9-inch, 180-pound object crashes into an irresistable 6-foot 11-inch, 275-pound force, the little guy is going to get hurt, right? On this play Norman Van Lier stole the ball from Bob Lanier, and Lanier accidentally pushed me aside during the resulting action. I went reeling backward, and suddenly Dave Bing came hurtling through the air and knocked me against the basket supports. I must have been hit in the spleen during the crash because at the end of the third quarter I had to stop the game, run off the court and go to the bathroom. It was only the second time in my officiating career that a visit to the lavatory took precedence over a basketball game.

Once again Jake and I worked without complications. After the game he told me that he had never been happier with a partner in his career, and I agreed that it went the same way with me. The personal tensions have disappeared. As Jake said, we have proved that two men can agree on the court even though we may disagree about things off the court.

Tuesday, April 2 (Off-day)

On the flight back to New York one of the stewardesses asked me if I knew Jim Barnett, the guard who has, during his nomadic career, played for Boston, San Diego, Portland and now Golden State. She said that she had known Barnett at the University of Oregon. "Yes, I know Mr. Barnett," I said to her. "Is he still flaky?" she asked. Yep, we were talking about the same Jim Barnett. I laughed and told her one of my Jim Barnett stories. One night Barnett, in the best tradition of the Hollywood stuntman, staggered out of bounds in an attempt to convince a referee that he had been forced out by an opponent. But the official rightfully called the violation on Barnett and gave the ball to the opposition. Incensed, Barnett punted the basketball fifty yards into the balcony. After watching the ball disappear into the seats, both referees turned to Barnett to eject him from the game, but they were too late—he was already en route to his dressing room. After the game Barnett knocked on the door to the officials' room and apologized for his punting display. Despite his apology, Barnett was informed that in accordance with league rules the kick would cost him $500. "Well, it was worth it!" Barnett said as he walked out the door. "That's something I always wanted to do."

I wish I had been there to see it. If the game was one-sided at the time, I probably would have given the signal for a field goal.

Thursday, April 4 (Milwaukee at Los Angeles)

After losing the first two games in Milwaukee, the Lakers beat the the Bucks here the other night, and the frantic Forum faithful no doubt expected another triumph tonight. What happened, instead, was a Milwaukee blowout as the Bucks ran off to an early 40-point lead and crushed the Lakers mercilessly. The game was televised coast-to-coast, but I'm sure that the people back east switched channels halfway into the second quarter. The Bucks did a lot of verbal complaining in their loss here, according to the word I received from Paul Mihalak, our alternate official. But in this game they were like a junior varsity team at Southside High, cheering each other on for 48 minutes.

Gail Goodrich hit only one field goal for the Lakers, and Happy Hairston attempted only five shots. Only Elmore Smith played well for Los Angeles, but then I had to eject Mr. Smith for mouthing the magic word to me. According to the rule known as the "tactile touch," defensive players can feel or touch their opponents above the waist. Gently, that is. Actually, it is a stupid rule that has become the bane of a referee's existence. It's one of the toughest judgment calls we have to make in a game. I remember one night I called a foul on Gus Johnson of the Bullets for holding on defense. Gus argued vehemently that he was just touching his opponent. "How do you know I'm holding?" he said to me. "Simple, Gus," I said. "The muscles in your arm were popping."

Smith was playing against Jabbar and at one point Jabbar faked to his right, rolled to his left, and caught one of Smith's elbows in his back. Listen. You cannot play a "tactile touch" by inserting your left elbow between an opponent's shoulder blades. I called a foul on Smith.

"What for?" he screamed.

"Get your elbow out of his back," I said. Then he called me the magic word—and was gone.

"Don't you dare call me that," I told him as he walked off the floor.

It's time the players found another expression to use when they want to release their frustrations. What about "shucks"? Or "gol danged?" How about "Dad gummit?"

I really like these coast-to-coast TV games from Los Angeles. They start the games at 7:00 P.M. rather than the usual 8:00 P.M., and they're usually finished by 9:15 or so, which leaves me plenty of time to catch the 11:00 P.M. red-eye special back to New York. Normally I have to rush like hell to catch the red-eye. Tonight, I had time for a Double D at the airport lounge.

Saturday, April 6 (Boston at Buffalo)

There is a Catholic Youth Organization convention here and some two thousand kids apparently spent the night roaming the lobby and the corridors in search of another party. Luckily for me I didn't arrive in town until this morning, having managed to get a good night's sleep in Greenwich. Jake O'Donnell came in last night, and when I saw him this morning he looked exhausted. "Damn kids," he said.

It was my first time back in Buffalo since L'Affaire Ranallo a month ago, and the first thing I did this morning was reach for the telephone directory. Last month, in fact, the day after Mr. Ranallo's down-with-Richie Powers column, a certain Mr. Frank Spinner of Buffalo wrote a letter to Walter Kennedy complaining about my capabilities as a referee and stating that he agreed 100 percent with Mr. Ranallo's story. The letter was forwarded to me, as all letters, pro and con, are mailed to the involved official. I did not think Mr. Spinner knew what he was talking about, so I wrote to him and told him so. I said he had a right to express his opinions about the Buffalo Braves and about the competency of Richie Powers at any time, and I also said he had a perfect right to jeer the referees at any time. I also suggested that for him to agree with the charges stated in the newspaper column was ludicrous. I described the various situations in the Buffalo-Seattle game, and how I handled them. Finally, I told Mr. Spinner that I'd like to meet him, and I invited him to be my guest at the game the next time I worked in Buffalo.

There was only one Frank Spinner listed in the telephone directory, so I dialed the number. "Frank," I said to the male voice that answered the call, "this is Richie Powers."

"Who?" the voice at the other end asked.

"Richie Powers, the referee," I said. The voice indicated no awareness of who or what Richie Powers was. "Is this Frank R. Spinner?" I said.

"No, this is Frank K. Spinner."

I explained the story to him.

"Oh, that's all right, Mr. Powers," Frank K. Spinner said. "If you can't find the other Mr. Spinner, I'll be glad to take the tickets."

In the dressing room before the game I showed the letter from Frank R. Spinner to Jake O'Donnell. "Maybe Frank R. Spinner is the pen name for a player in the league," Jake joked.

To my surprise, the real Frank R. Spinner appeared as Jake and I were walking from the dressing room to the court. "Hey, Richie," a voice said, "I'm Spinner."

Mr. Spinner was a stocky 5-foot 10-inch man about my age. I shook hands with and told him I had tried to reach him on the phone but got another Frank Spinner. "I can't talk now," I said, "but I'll see you after the game." At halftime of the Braves-Celtics game there was a knock on our door, and there was Spinner, standing quietly in the hallway. I motioned for him to come in.

"Thanks," he said. Mr. Spinner explained that he was a lawyer, a season-ticket holder and a basketball fanatic. "I just want you to know that I watched the first half with a different perspective and that I understand your problems a helluva lot better than I did a month ago. You guys don't have an easy job, I can see that now." I thanked Mr. Spinner for his kind comments, and he left. Jake and I looked at each other and shrugged our shoulders. Mr. Spinner's not falling in love with referees, I don't think, but at least he knows our job a little better than he did before.

The Buffalo-Boston game that Mr. Spinner saw was one of the best games I have ever worked. Not from the standpoint of officiating. I'm talking about the quality of the play, the excitement of the capacity crowd, the unbelievable pressure and tension, the conduct of the coaches—everything. Bob McAdoo gave a spectacular exhibition of shooting, Ernie DiGregorio proved that all rookies don't develop butterflies under pressure, John Havlicek was John Havlicek, Dave Cowens was Dave Cowens, and you couldn't ask for anything more. McAdoo is one of those rare NBA players who hardly says anything on the court. In fact, I can't remember the last time he registered a complaint about anything.

The score remained close throughout, with neither team able to mount a decisive surge, but despite the tension we had only one minor problem with each coach. Early in the game O'Donnell called a routine foul on one of the Braves that for some inexplicable reason prompted Jack Ramsay to walk to center court and make his Papal gesture. "Jack," I said to Ramsay, "I understand the pressure of this game for you, but this game doesn't mean a helluva lot for Jake and me, so stay on the bench and keep your cool." Ramsay was the model of perfect behavior the rest of the game.

At the beginning of the second half, Heinsohn reacted to a foul against the Celtics by waving his hands in disgust, and I had to tell him the same thing I had told Ramsay.

In the end the whole game came down to the last 20 seconds. Buffalo, trailing the series two games to one, had the ball and a 2-point lead, 94 to 92. As play resumed following a Braves time out, I noticed Paul Silas of the Celtics grabbing Ernie D. so I promptly called a foul on Silas. But, Jake was also blowing his whistle at the same time. I figured he was calling the same thing, a foul on Silas. But Jake was waving his hands and indicating that Buffalo had called a time out before the Silas foul. In other words, the foul I had called on Silas was wiped out by the Buffalo time out.

After the time out, Ernie D. threw the ball to Jim McMillian, who caught it easily and put it onto the floor. Suddenly, the red-headed giant in the Boston uniform swooped through the air, batted the ball to Don Chaney who passed it to Havlicek for a twenty-foot jump shot that tied the game at 94-all. Stunned by the sudden turn of events, Buffalo again called time out to set up a possible game-winning shot. During the time out Heinsohn called me over and said: "Richie, if they miss the shot and we get the rebound, we'll call an immediate time out." In other words, Heinsohn was telling me that he wanted no ticks on the clock. Fine. However, Boston had to have possession of the ball before calling time out.

The Braves got the ball in-bounds once more and, with five seconds left, McAdoo, who had not missed a shot in about an hour, tried a jumper from the top of the key. I was under the basket, a position that afforded me a perfect view of the large game clock behind the basket at the other end of the court. McAdoo and that clock were almost perfectly in line, and I could see the clock ticking down to zero. Why every arena in the NBA doesn't have a similar clock arrangement, I don't know. McAdoo's shot missed, and the ball bounced off the side of the rim. Suddenly, to my left, there was McMillian standing all alone because Cowens had gamely tried to block McAdoo's shot out deep. McMillian leaped into the air, and grabbed the loose ball when there were exactly two seconds left on the clock. Calmly, some people thought too calmly, McMillian took a half step, laid the ball against the backboard and watched it drop through the netting. I was watching, too, and the ball was en route from the rim to the floor as the clock read "0:00."

I never heard the horn ending the game. However, Jake signaled that the basket was good, and I signaled that the game was over by waving my hands in front of my body and crossing them a number of times.

"Richie!" John Havlicek yelled, "there's still one second." "No," I said firmly. "It's over." And I pointed to the clock. Havlicek protested that the horn had not sounded. "That doesn't make any difference," I said. I waved my hands again in an emphatic gesture to indicate to one and all that the game was over, that Buffalo had won—and, of course, that the series was squared at two games apiece. Heinsohn was livid, but he calmed down when I repeated the exact time sequence of the play to him.

After the game I found out that the CBS-TV play-by-play man, Don Criqui, had interpreted my hand-waving to mean that the basket was no good and that the game would be going into overtime. So, in fact, did a lot of other people in Buffalo. I wish people knew more about our business. I don't make the call for a basket or a non-basket while I'm standing under the boards. The trail referee calls the shot good or not good—not the lead referee. Jake called the basket good. It was open-and-shut. Listen. I wouldn't nullify a basket from my position under the hoop unless my partner suddenly collapsed at center court. I was waving my hands to signify that the game was over. That was my job.

Sunday, April 7 (Los Angeles at Milwaukee)

Jake and I watched the Bullets-Knicks game at our hotel here in Milwaukee, and we felt for Bob Rakel and Earl Strom because it was a very difficult game for them to control. Neither the Bullets nor the Knicks played consistently, and there was a lot of violence under both boards as players fought for the rebounds of missed shots. On one play the television cameras showed a replay of Phil Chenier of the Bullets taking a swing and hitting Clyde Frazier of the Knicks. Bob and Earl obviously did not see Chenier's swing because they did not call any fouls.

"Oh-oh," I said. "Watch Frazier get even with Chenier."

On the next play Clyde took the ball, went head-to-head against Chenier, gave him a million head, body and leg fakes and scored an easy basket. Chenier's actions aroused Frazier so much that Clyde, who had been playing somewhat lethargically, led the Knicks to victory in overtime.

The Bucks expected some trouble from the Lakers, particularly after the embarrassment that Los Angeles suffered back home last Thursday night. In fact, at the pre-game meetings with the captains at center court, Gail Goodrich of the Lakers informed Oscar Robertson of the Bucks that "we have come to play tonight." The score was 6 to 6 after a few minutes, and then, before the Lakers knew what had hit them, it was 26 to 6 for the Bucks. Kareem Abdul-Jabbar was immense, scoring and rebounding almost at will, and the Bucks played very cohesively as they eliminated the

Lakers in five games. At the end I shook hands with Jim Price and some of the other Lakers, and we all gave each other that wide-eyed nod that says "See ya next year." I hope I'll be seeing Jerry West next year, too.

Tuesday, April 9 (Detroit at Chicago)

Before the start of the Chicago-Detroit game, Pat Summerall joked: "I hope you guys aren't going to bring us bad luck again." I *think* he was joking. What Pat meant was that CBS didn't want another blowout like the Lakers-Bucks game that Jake and I worked last week in Los Angeles. For a time, though, it appeared that the Powers-O'Donnell jinx was still very much alive. Playing before a noisy home crowd, the Bulls stormed to a 30-plus point lead by the early moments of the second quarter. Bob Love of the Bulls was hotter than firewater, while the Pistons were colder than the ice cubes I like in my Double Ds.

The NBA has a rule that states that each team must call one mandatory time out in each period, and for television games the referee calls a third mandatory time out in each period for commercials. As a general rule in televised games, these time outs are planned to take place at the 2 1/2-, 6 1/2- and 9 1/2-minute mark in each period. Well, we had a foul-up tonight in the second quarter when Detroit had to call a time out with 8:42 to play in order to reorganize in the face of the Chicago onslaught. By the time matters were sorted out, the three mandatory time outs had been called and there were still 6:50 left to play. Dick Motta graciously came to our rescue by agreeing to be charged with a second Chicago time out that he didn't have to take. At the time Chicago was leading by 25 or 30 points, and CBS got its commercial.

What happened, naturally, was that Detroit began to find the basket. Suddenly the Pistons narrowed the Bulls lead to 10 points, and Motta was standing on the sidelines and giving me holy hell. Why? He wanted that time out he had taken earlier. In a fit of anger I finally said, "Shut up!" I realized I should not have said it the moment the words were out of my mouth. At halftime Motta came over to me and said, "Richie, you embarrassed me." I had, and I apologized. However, Dick had agreed to take the time out, and it wasn't my fault that he was second-guessing himself.

Detroit maintained its strong surge the rest of the game and eventually tied the score as Bob Lanier manhandled the rebounds and Dave Bing scored the way Love had scored in the early stages. In the end, however, the Bulls squeeked out a slim victory and took a 3–2 lead in the series. Detroit had a chance to tie the score at the final buzzer, but a Bing shot just fell short. Afterwards, Detroit Coach Ray Scott stopped Jake and me and congratulated us on a great game. We appreciated his comment even more because it came from the losing coach.

"Ray," I said, "you know what makes this game great? It's people like you making comments like that. And it's a team like the Pistons that won't quit when it's down by thirty points on the other team's court."

Oh, yeah. I hope CBS was happy, too.

Wednesday, April 10 (New York at Capital)

I called Johnny Nucatola and said that the only bad thing about the Chicago-Detroit game was my statement to Dick Motta. I also told him I had apologized to Motta for my comments.

Later that day Nucatola met Ginger and me at LaGuardia Airport, and we all took the shuttle to Washington for tonight's sixth game of the Capital–New York series. During our conversation Johnny mentioned that Jake O'Donnell had called him before the start of the playoffs to suggest that the O'Donnell-Powers team be broken up even before it ever had a chance to work together. In blunt language, Jake had advised Johnny that O'Donnell and Powers simply did not get along and that both of us would be better off working with someone else. I was hardly surprised by Nucatola's revelation because Jake had told me the same thing. Well, what I didn't know was that Jake also had called Johnny after the second playoff game to apologize for his earlier suggestion. I may be belaboring the point, but even in this profession one must learn to overcome antipathies and animosities. And right now Jake and I are getting along absolutely perfectly.

Nucatola then advised me that he had received a complaint from Bill Bradley and Earl Monroe of the Knicks about the height of the baskets at the new Capital Centre, and asked me to check the height and the level of both baskets before the game. The New York complaint reminded me of an old Red Auerbach story.

One night before a playoff game in Cincinnati Auerbach told me that one of his players thought the baskets were too low. "Okay, Red, I'll get a ten-foot pole and check them." I asked the maintenance man at the Cincinnati Gardens if he had a ten-foot pole. "Yeah, it's lying right there," he said, pointing to a long pole. So I picked up the pole, walked out onto the court and set it under the basket. Sure enough, the rim of the basket was about one foot higher than the pole. "How the hell do these things happen?" I yelled at no one in particular. The capacity crowd, all the players and the two coaches were laughing like hell. Then I looked at the pole. "Get me a tape measure," I commanded. The maintenance man produced a tape and I stretched it along the pole. Would you believe that the pole measured nine feet? I threw the pole down and ordered the maintenance man to produce a ten-foot pole—"or else." Or else? Anyway, he produced a ten-foot pole, and the baskets, despite what one of the Celtics happened to think, were exactly ten feet above the floor.

When I measured the baskets tonight, they were in perfect order. I put a level to both rims, and they were flat.

Nucatola had suggested I make the basket checks overtly, so I waited until the pre-game warm-up was completed before calling for the paraphernalia. The capacity crowd must have thought I was a crackpot. In fact, while I was perched on top of the ladder with the level in my hands one fan yelled, "Dunk the little bastard!"

For three quarters the Bullets and the Knicks tore at each other like snipers. Dave DeBusschere collected three quick personals and went to the bench, while Kevin Porter of the Bullets picked up two early fouls and went to the verbiage.

"Young man," I said to Porter, "you're a vital cog to your team, and if you lose your cool again, you're liable to get thrown out of here."

Porter was stunned by my comments. "Mr. Powers, I . . ." he started.

"Mr. *Powers?*" I interrupted. "Kevin, you've been calling me Richie all year. What's with the formalities now?"

Once the fourth quarter began the Bullets, trailing the series three games to two and facing elimination, rallied from a 7-point deficit, with good help from Kevin Porter, and bombed the Knicks off the court to win the game, tie the series and force a seventh game up in New York on Friday night.

Friday, April 12 (Capital at New York)

There is no question in my mind that the Knicks owe some part of their series-clinching victory over the Bullets tonight to the 19,694 basketball "nuts" who hollered and cheered everything the Knicks did for more than two hours on the court. At the same time, they jeered and booed everything the Bullets did or didn't do. Before the game John Condon, the P.A. man, introduced the N.Y. team to the crowd, and each Knick received a standing ovation that lasted for at least a minute. The Bullets? Standing boos. It's funny. Down at the Capital Centre the crowd seemed to be

(185)

50–50 for the Knicks and the hometown Bullets.

Jake seemed a little tense in the dressing room before the game; I don't think he had ever worked a seventh game before. Once the game began, it seemed as if everyone had the seventh-game jitters. For a long stretch in the first period the Knicks and the Bullets played like a bunch of kids who had never met each other and didn't know whether to kick, throw or shoot the ball. However, once the nervousness wore off, we had a super game. And, as expected, there were a few minor flare-ups. Dean Meminger of the Knicks was defending against Archie Clark at one point and using his hands on Clark like a piston. Bang! Bang! Bang! went Meminger's hands, snapping against Clark's hips. I called a foul on Meminger, and he looked at me with innocent surprise. "Touch him, don't punch him," I said. Meminger's idea of the "tactile touch" was hardly a touch. When I called the foul, Clark nodded his head. In doing so, he acknowledged that he now knew the "tactile touch" was not a one-way street. In the sixth game I had called a foul on Clark for doing exactly what Meminger did in this game, and he protested the foul at great lengths. Now he knows that I wasn't out to get him, that I was calling what I saw.

Early in the fourth quarter Elvin Hayes went up for a stuff shot against Dave DeBusschere, but as he was jumping up his left hand snaked out and knocked DeBusschere's hands away from the ball. Offensive foul on Hayes. A couple of minutes later Hayes was defending under the basket when Clyde Frazier drove the lane. As Frazier went up his left arm was out, as it always is when he's driving the lane. But he never moved it as an offensive weapon. Frazier's shot went in, and suddenly there was Hayes staggering across the end line and falling to the floor. I had seen no contact. I gave the "safe" sign, telling him there had been no foul. The Bullets promptly called time out and Captain Wes Unseld came over to protest Frazier's basket. Unseld said that he couldn't understand how I called Hayes for an offensive foul on the same type of play that I had just allowed Frazier to execute without any whistle. "It might have looked like the same play," I said to Unseld, "but you know and I know that it wasn't." The Bullets were trying to swindle an official. If a referee is out of position on a play, he might get caught in such a swindle, but I was in good position to see both plays. There were at least six inches between Frazier's outstretched arm and the Bullets' emblem on Hayes' shirt.

In the end it was hardly a good night for Mr. Hayes or the Bullets. Hayes was held to 12 points as lanky John Gianelli swarmed all over him, forcing him into bad shots and boxing him neatly away from the boards. And the Bullets, who trailed by only two points—57 to 55—at the half, scored only 26 points during the rest of the game and ultimately lost by the score of 91 to 81.

Actually, the 10-point difference was misleading, because it was a 3-point game until the final minute. As Jake and I walked off, Hayes gave me one final verbal blast and said that we had taken the game away from the Bullets. He incorporated the magic word in his comments and I will report his conduct to the league office in the morning. The tragedy of sports, though, is that someone has to lose, and the taste of defeat is very bitter, indeed. I empathize with losers, because referees have the same problem. No matter how good we are, when we walk off the court, some people think we failed. In fact, the only people happy with Jake O'Donnell and Richie Powers tonight probably were Jake O'Donnell and Richie Powers.

Back in the dressing room I admitted to Nucatola that I had made one blatant mistake on a relatively incidental play. Listen. I can't alibi every tough call by saying, "Okay, I might have missed it." On the particular play I gave the ball to the Bullets, thinking that it had gone out of bounds off Bill Bradley. Actually, it had gone out off Phil Chenier —not Bradley—so I should have given the ball to the Knicks. On another heavily debated out-of-bounds play, though I knew I was 100 percent correct, despite what Dave DeBusschere may still think. The ball went out of bounds off one of the Knicks, not one of the Bullets, as DeBusschere insisted. Dave explained his view of the play to me, and I explained my view to him. "If you're right, then I kicked hell out of it," I told DeBusschere. "But you're not right. I called it correctly."

We were still unwinding, sipping a beer, when Paul Mihalak rushed in with the information that the Boston Celtics had just closed out the Buffalo Braves in the sixth game of their series, 106 to 104, as Jo Jo White made the game-and-series winning foul shots after time had expired. So now the Celtics play the Knicks in a seven-game rematch of last year's great series for the Eastern Division Championship.

Saturday, April 13 (Off-day)

I talked with Johnny Nucatola this morning, and we spent a half hour rehashing the play that ultimately won the game last night for Boston. With time running out and the score tied, John Havlicek of the Celtics missed a shot, but then White grabbed the rebound, went up for a shot and was knocked to the floor by Two-for-McAdoo as the clock reached 0:00. Darrell Garretson made the call on McAdoo, a very gutty call, I might add, although referees never think of the consequences of the calls they make. They call what they see regardless of when, where, why or how it happens. The last thought of any referee, at any time is, "Hell, maybe I'd better let it go."

Johnny told me that Buffalo has protested the game and has threatened legal action to prevent the first game of the Boston–New York series scheduled for tomorrow afternoon up in Boston. Legal action my eye. The game films definitely showed that McAdoo had fouled White on the play. The Buffalo people claim that the clock had reached 0:00 before the foul was called, but the films prove that the clock was still running when White went up for the shot. The Braves then turned around and protested the game on the basis that 1 second still should have been left on the clock for them to try one long game-tying shot.

Listen. When a clock reads "1" second, it is never more than one second. It could be 1/10 of a second or 1/5 of a second. That's how clocks work. Time, in other words, is somewhere between 1 and o. So, at "o", there is no time left. What a way to end a season. But while the Braves lost the game, they bordered on beating Boston in each and every game they lost. In fact, I suspect that Buffalo won three out of every four periods in every game against the Celtics. That other period killed them. Some day their time will come, and I, for one, don't think that time is very far away.

Tuesday, April 16 (Chicago at Milwaukee)

The league office is so happy with the combination of O'Donnell and Powers during the first round of the playoffs that it has scrapped a plan to change the officiating teams for the semifinals and will continue to use us in tandem on a regular basis. Great!

I flew into Milwaukee early this morning. Nucatola called me at the hotel in midafternoon and said he wanted to meet with Jake, alternate referee Bob Rakel and me as soon as possible about the Dennis Awtrey–Kareem Abdul Jabbar feud that has been dominating the sports pages of the local newspapers the past few days. It seems that when the Bucks met the Bulls in their last regular-season game, Awtrey and Jabbar had a minor scuffle in which Dennis hit Kareem with a punch. And now the papers are making the Awtrey-Jabbar battle sound like the fight of the century. Listen. Awtrey and Jabbar always have had very physical battles in their games that I have worked, but Awtrey has never been more physical against Jabbar than Nate Thurmond has, or Dave

Cowens or Willis Reed. Dennis does have a quick temper, though.

Talk of the Awtrey-Jabbar battle reminded me of an Atlanta–Los Angeles playoff series several years ago when the Hawks were still playing their games at Alexander Hall on the campus of Georgia Tech, where the basketball floor was harder than concrete. After 48 minutes on that Georgia Tech floor I always felt as though my pelvic bones were lost in my arm pits. Anyway, I was watching the first game of the series on television and the Lakers rallied to win by a half-dozen points. I saw nothing unusual in the game. In fact, it looked as if Mendy Rudolph and Manny Sokol had maintained perfect control. The next day, though, the Atlanta papers were littered with stories in which Richie Guerin said the next game would be a "bloodbath." Guerin, the general manager and coach of the Hawks at the time, went on to make several other vicious statements that suggested Atlanta had lost the game because the referees had permitted the Lakers to beat up the Hawks. "Immediate retaliation," was promised by Guerin.

Well, I had been assigned to work the next L.A.–Atlanta game, and before I left home I received a call from Walter Kennedy. He told me that I should talk to the coaches and the captains before the game and tell them there will be no bloodbath—or else. Before the game I bumped into Guerin, an old friend from my years back in the Bronx, and he made a gesture to me that indicated his post-game comments following the loss to the Lakers were strictly for conversation, designed only to arouse his club from its lethargy. "It was newspaper talk, Richie," Guerin said, making a safe sign with his hands.

Still, I fulfilled the task given to me by Mr. Kennedy and called a meeting of the coaches and the captains. "Gentlemen," I said, "this game will be played according to the rules of the National Basketball Association. And there will be no bloodbath—or else." Bill Bridges, the captain of the Hawks, nodded his head. "Right," he said. "There will be no bloodbath around here because they have *him* on their side." Then Bridges pointed to Wilt Chamberlain, who was sitting pensively on the Lakers' bench. As Bridges said, as long as Los Angeles had the strongest player on its side, why fight it. Once the game began, the Hawks roared to 16- or 17-point lead at the half, but then were blown out by the Lakers after intermission. And there wasn't one finger waved in anger the whole night.

I went down to the coffee shop for the meeting with Nucatola, who wanted to discuss the positioning of the lead referee under the basket. It seems that in the fourth Los Angeles–Milwaukee game that Jake and I worked out on the coast, there was a play Johnny had seen on TV where Jabbar faked to his right, rolled to his left, then threw out an elbow that knocked Elmore Smith away. To Nucatola's amazement, no foul was called on Jabbar.

John said that Jake—the trail referee—should have been in position to make the call. I told John that it was my mistake, that I should have been in better position to get a good angle on the play. Jake and I feel the lead referee should take a position slightly to the right of the basket. Jabbar normally plays the pivot so that the basket is slightly to the right of his left shoulder when he stands with his back to the basket. In other words, Jabbar operates from what is the right side of the lane as the referee looks up the court. The lead referee, then, would be almost directly behind Jabbar and his defender. From this position, we can adjust to let the defenders know we are looking at them when they are working on Jabbar and pressuring him with their hands and legs. And we can also observe all the shirt-grabbing that they do against Jabbar.

The problem with this position, though, is that when Jabbar rolls to his left, the lead referee occasionally loses sight of some of the tactics used not only by the defender but also by Jabbar himself. So the trail referee must watch the arms of the defender and also Jabbar. It's as difficult as it sounds. John listened and then said that he wants the lead referee to take a position to the left of the basket, not the right, as he looks back up the court. So we will try that tonight, and see what happens.

John also said he wants me to get the coaches and captains together before the game and more or less repeat the speech I made in Atlanta a few years ago. From the way he spoke, though, I could tell that he was not convinced that this was the route to take. "John," I said, "I'm not going to make any speeches. What I'll do is greet the coaches and the captains and wish them good luck in a normal way. I think that will let them know that Jake and I will be handling the game and keeping it under good control at all times."

Before the game I met Larry Costello, the Milwaukee coach, and said "Good luck" to him. While I was waiting for Dick Motta, the Chicago coach, to come onto the court, Nucatola came down from the stands and told me to check the Chicago team's bench. According to league rules, only the coaches, the players and the trainer may sit on the bench during a game. The Bulls, though, had brought their team physician, Dr. David Bachman, to Milwaukee for the series, and he was occupying a seat on the bench. I don't like to force these minor issues, but we must treat everyone alike. I walked to the bench and informed the doctor that he would have to sit elsewhere. He was very gracious and promptly got a chair and took a position just behind and to the right of the bench. Motta, who likes to delay his arrival until the last possible moment, had appeared by that time, and I extended him the same "good luck" wish that I had offered to Costello.

Then, at the pre-game meeting of the captains, I announced: "Gentlemen, this is like a regular-season game for us."

And it was. It was a quick and quiet game that Milwaukee won easily as the Bulls struggled along without the leadership that Jerry Sloan normally gives them. Sloan has ripped a tendon in his foot and will not play in this series. I, for one, don't believe that Chicago can beat Milwaukee without

Sloan's aggressiveness, shooting, ball-hawking and pick-ing. Jerry sets up probably the meanest pick in the league, taking a kamikaze attitude as he stands in the way of big forwards and bigger centers. I think he'd be a helluva tight end or defensive end—or both.

Afterwards, one of the Chicago players joked that the game could have been refereed by a couple of scoutmas-ters. We only called ten fouls in the first half, and not many more in the second. Dennis Awtrey was booed the minute he arrived on the court. There were signs all over town, and throughout the arena, that said Awtrey was everything from a bum to a zoo-monster. Awtrey fouled Jabbar a couple of times, but they were the standard types of fouls, nothing premeditated or violent. But Awtrey was the ogre as far as the Milwaukee fans were concerned, and the only time they cheered him was when he missed a shot. After the game Awtrey claimed that the "close calls by the officials affected my performance." Cripes! Awtrey played 24 minutes, col-lected only two fouls, and made only two of the six shots he attempted. Players can do anything they want on the basketball court. They can play with fouls, or without fouls. They can play physically, or passively. Under pressure, though, they always seem to relate their problems to the way the game was officiated. I'm used to that.

Jabbar, on the other hand, complimented us for "letting us all play basketball."

After the game one of the local television announcers asked me how Jake and I had felt before the game in re-sponse to the pressures and tensions that had been build-ing up between the Bucks and the Bulls. "The referees didn't feel any differently about this game than a game we worked back in February," I said. "These stories never bother us." It's really weird. A momentary flare-up that occurred six weeks ago suddenly becomes a minor *cause célèbre* in the press and on TV. In the playoffs, people tend to make mountains out of molehills. And that's not an original thought. By the way, Jake and I tried Johnny

Nucatola's suggested position under the basket, and while it did not offer any real complications, it was uncomfortable. In the end we were alternating our positions under the basket. Come to think of it, that may be the real solution. Maybe the players know where a referee always likes to be on the court and have learned how to take advantage of the referee's position. This game's a never-ending battle of wits.

On the flight to New York Pat Summerall told me that Red Auerbach recently admitted that the Celtics always held pre-game meetings to discuss the referees. Auerbach obviously knows and understands the idiosyncracies of many officials in the NBA. No doubt he knows "we can do this" or "we can't do this" with Richie Powers. On the other hand, I know the idiosyncracies of many coaches, many players and many general managers, so it's a two-way street. Hey, if you know the cop on the corner will let you halfway stop at a stop sign, then that's what you're going to do. Right? Right! Who's kidding whom? No one!

Thursday, April 18 (Off-day)

On this delightful spring day, a time when my mind is thinking about the end of the basketball season in a few weeks and the beginning of my annual campaign to become a respectable golfer instead of a shanking hacker, I would like to list my favorite pet peeves about conditions and other things in the NBA. Serious things, mind you. No frivolity here.

(1) Smoking should be prohibited in every arena in the NBA. They have outlawed smoking in Boston, Phoenix and some other cities, but not in Madison Square Garden, the Milwaukee Arena and most other buildings. When I work in a building where people are smoking, the smoke burns my eyes and bothers my breathing. And I'm sure that

if it bothers me it must bother the players.

(2) I normally arrive at the actual site of a game at least an hour before the opening tap-off. What bothers me when I arrive is the sight of players of both teams warming up at the same basket. It's unprofessional, to say the least. I don't believe in fraternization of any sort once the players have entered the arena. I have suggested many times in the past that if players want to warm-up long before gametime, they should use opposite ends of the court, but nothing has ever been done to correct the situation.

(3) Why should referees walk onto the court five minutes before game time and see the opposing coaches sitting on the same bench and chatting amiably? If you ask me, this, too, is unprofessional. The public is watching. And so are the referees. Coaches can, and should, conduct their pre-game seminars out of sight of the crowd. Then again, maybe only a pristine shanking hacker like myself notices things like this.

(4) The most ridiculous thing in basketball is the seating situation on team benches during the playing of the games. It seems that the coach and the trainer always sit at one end, and the non-playing players sit way down the other end. The gap looks ridiculous. Most teams consist of about fifteen people: a coach, an assistant coach, a trainer and twelve players. Of course, five players are always on the floor, working in the game. So there are at least five empty places on the bench. And those five empty seats are between the men in uniform and the men in mufti. Let's have some team togetherness. Eliminate the seat gap. Instead of providing fifteen seats on the bench, why not provide ten? Sure, it's not a major problem, but it shows how my mind works.

(5) Let's legalize the zone or stop complaining to the officials about it. All teams play some sort of a six- to eight-foot legal zone against certain offenses. It hasn't hurt the game, and with the abilities of the players, plus the 24-

second clock, and the great fan interest that has developed, changing the rule wouldn't hurt in my view.

In any event, I've said my piece.

Friday, April 19 (New York at Boston)

Facing the likely prospect of falling behind the Celtics three games to zip, the Knicks roared out tonight and played spectacular basketball for three quarters en route to a convincing lead of some 20 points. The New York players looked like a bunch of demons when they appeared on the Boston Garden court—in fact, Bill Bradley's eyebrows even seemed to be pointed up. Walt Frazier played as though he was planted on Cloud Nine, scoring 34 points during the first three quarters in which the Knicks literally rolled over the befuddled Bostonians.

Then, as they do so often, the Celtics surged from behind at the start of the fourth quarter, suddenly playing the way the Knicks had played during the first three periods. They contained Frazier, keeping him away from the ball, and Cowens, who had more or less been a spectator in the early stages, began to play keepaway with the rebounds. The Celtics out-rebounded the Knicks 20 to 3 during the final 12 minutes. And so, with 34 seconds to play, the Celtics had cut their deficit from 20 points to just 2—100 to 98—and had the ball in the New York end. Havlicek forced a shot, but the ball fell short. Don Chaney recovered the rebound, but Bill Bradley intercepted Chaney's pass up court. Jo Jo White immediately fouled Bradley, who made the two free throws and increased the Knicks lead to 102 to 98. Seconds later Don Nelson of the Celtics converted two free throws himself, narrowing the Boston deficit back to two points— 102 to 100. Now there were three seconds showing on the clock as the Knicks called time out. Three seconds, remember, means anything from 2.1 seconds to 3.0 seconds on the clock. Thinking about the scene in Buffalo a few weeks ago, I walked over and reminded Tommy Heinsohn that there were not necessarily a full three seconds left to play in the game. He nodded his head. On the in-bounds play New York fired the ball to John Gianelli in the deep corner, and Gianelli promptly was fouled by Silas. Right away I looked at the clock and it read: 0:01. Heinsohn was standing along the sidelines and screaming his head off. "Tommy, I told you about the clock," I said. "It took a full second-plus for everything to happen, I know that." He nodded, and returned to the bench. Gianelli had two chances, and he missed the first shot. Regardless what Gianelli did with his second shot, Boston, of course, wanted to call an immediate time out the instant one of the Celtics touched the ball. "Tommy," I said to Heinsohn, "I know you're going to call time out if he misses, but remember that you must have possession of the ball first. I won't react until one of your guys gets possession, if he does."

On missed foul shots, the clock does not start again until a player touches the ball once it has bounced away from the basket. A player, mind you. Nothing else. Gianelli missed his second free throw. The ball bounced high into the air, then one of the Celtics snatched it and screamed time out. And I was saying "one thousand and"—never reaching the one—when I signaled for the time out. A fraction of a second later the buzzer went off. No way. The game was not over. Indeed, Boston had the ball with something less than a second to play. Time enough to score a basket? The Knicks, were running off the court, but Jake put up his hands to stop the cavalry charge and informed Red Holzman that there was still one second to play.

"Why?" Holzman asked.

"The time out beat the horn," I said. "It was an obvious fact."

When they put the ball back into play, the Celtics tried to lob a long pass to Cowens, who, in turn, tried to redirect the ball into the basket. However, the ball bounced off Cowens' hands, and the game ended. Listen to this. When

Cowens touched the ball, I began to count off the last second and, unbelievably, I counted "one thousand and one, one thou—" before the game-ending horn went off.

It was a confusing night. Earlier in the week Johnny Nucatola had criticized me for not pointing in some direction on all out-of-bounds calls. In the past I have simply called the color of the team that will get the ball—I never have pointed in the direction that the ball will go. So tonight I tried to conquer that little chink in my armor and pointed in some direction each and every time the ball went out of bounds. Then there was a play under the basket, and the ball bounced out of bounds off Don Nelson's head. I pointed back over my shoulder. I assumed that Nelson was defending on the play, and I was pointing in the direction I thought the Knicks were moving. However, Nelson was attacking the basket, not defending it, so I had pointed in the wrong direction.

"Whose ball is it?" asked Clyde Frazier, looking a little surprised.

"You're ball, of course," I said.

"Then what're you pointing that way for?" Frazier said, looking befuddled.

"What way?" I said.

"That way," he said, pointing in Boston's direction.

"Well, what way are you going?" I said.

"Thataway," he said, pointing the other way.

"Well, that's the way we're going," I said.

It was the longest conversation I've ever had with Clyde. It also served as a perfect example of why I don't like to point during a game. If I call the team's color, the players should be able to straighten out the direction they're going by themselves.

After the game I went back to the hotel, and what was on television? The complete replay of the Knicks-Celtics game that Jake and I had just worked. It was the first time I've ever seen myself in action for 48 minutes, and it made me think I ought to wear a rubber belt around my waist to keep it in. Rick Barry was doing the color commentary for CBS, and when I finally got the "pointing" play all straightened out and gave the ball to the Knicks, Barry said: "A good referee always admits his mistakes." Right on.

I was more interested in another play, though. On one maneuver Havlicek drove against Frazier and Earl Monroe. As I saw the play, I figured Havlicek would have to walk, but I never saw the walk because Monroe and Frazier crossed in front of me and obscured my vision just as Havlicek shot the ball through the basket. I half blew my whistle, or, rather, quarter blew it. What happened was that I tried to stop the whistle just after I started to blow it, and only the slightest shrill came out.

"Didn't I hear a slight peep?" Frazier had asked.

"Maybe you did," I said, "but I'm sorry. It was a slight inadvertent whistle that I tried to stop but was too late." He accepted my explanation without any comment. Clyde is that way. He's a reasonable individual. Well, on the CBS replay I saw that Havlicek did walk, and that I should have called him for walking. He had caught the ball with one foot on the floor, then took two more steps. According to the rules, if you catch a pass with one foot on the ground, then that's your first step, and you are allowed only one more step. Normally, what players do in such cases is sort of knock the ball ahead of them and then chase it, thus eliminating the possibility of a walking violation.

Saturday, April 20 (Off-day)

I watched the second half of the Milwaukee-Chicago game on television this afternoon, but I missed seeing Dick Motta get ejected for throwing his sport jacket on the floor. Motta's actions were predictable. He had to stimulate the Bulls in some way in order to get more action and firepower from his line-up. Without Sloan, the Bulls do not seem to have an on-court leader, a guy who makes things happen.

Motta pumped the Bulls up for a while—but not long enough.

The funniest moment in the game came when Benny the Bull, the mascot of the Chicago team, was ordered from the court by the officials. I don't know what Benny—a Chicago businessman who dresses up like a bull—said to them, but I know he didn't learn those words during his undergraduate days at Princeton. Yes, Benny the Bull is really a Tiger from Princeton.

Sunday, April 21 (Boston at New York)

The Madison Square Garden crowd greeted the Knicks with the same ear-shattering ovations that they accorded them before the start of the seventh game of the Capital series ten days ago, but this time the crowd could not help the Knicks. Maybe the Celtics played with cotton stuffed in their ears. They beat the Knicks 98 to 91 in a super game to take a seemingly insurmountable three-to-one lead in the series. And it was an exhausting afternoon for Misters O'Donnell and Powers. Dave Cowens and I had some problems in the early going when I called Cowens for walking, palming and 3-seconds in a span of about six minutes. People always ask me why we call so many violations on some people, and so few violations on others. Well, the answer is that the Cowenses and the Fraziers and the Havliceks have the ball more than most people.

The Celtics led almost throughout the game, but the Knicks closed to within 51 to 50 at the half when Earl Monroe threw in a back-to-the-basket blind shot that just beat the buzzer. In fact, the ball swished through the hoop a moment after the buzzer had sounded. Red Auerbach, who was sitting in a seat just behind the scorer's table, gave me some flak about Monroe's shot at the half. "Don't lose your equilibrium, Red," I said. As he walked away, he said a few more things, so I warned him again: "Don't lose your cool, Red." He looked at me and said, "Bullshit!" I shook my head. "That's going to the office," I said.

Most of the action occurred during the second half, and, unfortunately, I got things away to a bad start by making a terrible blunder. Oddly enough, as we sat in the dressing room during the intermission, I told Jake and Paul Mihalak, our alternate referee, that the first six minutes of the third quarter probably would be the killer, one way or the other. Perhaps my words made me overanxious once play resumed. Don Nelson grabbed a rebound to the left of the basket, about three feet away from Jake, who was the lead referee on the play. I was the trail referee, and I was standing about thirty feet away from Nelson. Controlling the ball, Nelson paused to shoot, and suddenly Bill Bradley came up from behind him and waved at the ball. I thought I saw Bradley slap Nelson's arm and I whistled for a foul. Everyone was mad at me, even Jake. There had not been any foul and I certainly should not have called it. It was a very amateurish thing to do, and, fortunately, something I don't do very often.

Bradley and Red Holzman yelled at me, and for a moment, at least, I wished I were someplace else. "One shot," I said. So then the Boston bench started to yell at me, claiming that Nelson was in the act of shooting and should get two shots. What I seemed to be doing, in effect, was rectifying one wrong by creating another wrong. Now both teams hated me, and I wasn't so certain that Jake didn't feel the same way. Actually, it was not an amelioration to give Nelson only one shot, because he was not in the act of shooting as far as I could tell. No matter. I was a happy man when the whole play was finished—and, hopefully, forgotten.

I had another difficult call on an out-of-bounds play. Nelson and John Gianelli scrambled for a loose ball, and while driving for the ball Nelson knocked it out of bounds. I pointed to Gianelli and said: "Your ball. White." The Knicks, of course, were wearing the home white uniforms.

Well, while pointing to Gianelli, I also was pointing in the direction that the Celtics were moving. There was some controversy for a few moments. The hell with it. I'm going back to the *color* call, and let the players figure out which way they're going.

The Celtics maintained their lead to the end, and with a few seconds to play they had the ball out near midcourt after a foul by Frazier. After calling a time out, they returned for the in-bounds pass and I planted Don Nelson in the proper position outside the court. The Knicks insisted that Nelson should throw the ball in-bounds from the division line at midcourt, but I positioned Nelson about four feet inside the division line, in the front court, because that was where Frazier had committed the foul. In positioning Nelson, I also enforced the three-foot rule for in-bounds passes; in other words, the defensive players must allow the in-bounds passer three feet of free space, because of the tight quarters around the Garden floor. Besides that, I had to start the clock with a hand signal, watch for encroachment by the defense, look for fouls, and make certain that the pass came directly in-bounds.

Over the years I have developed a technique to count to five seconds, which is the time the in-bounds passer is allotted to get the ball in play. I used to click my fingers, but the noise was too audible and distracting. So now I use my feet. I start the count with my left foot, which is one thousand and one, then continue on my right foot, which is one thousand and two. When my left foot hits the floor the third time, it means that five seconds have expired.

On this play the Knicks covered the Celtics perfectly, and Nelson had no outlet for the ball. As my right foot hit the floor for the second time, meaning that four seconds had elapsed since I gave Nelson the ball and signaled the play to begin, Nelson called another time out. The New York bench jumped up and shouted that Nelson had committed a violation, but I waved the Knicks off. No way did Nelson use up his five seconds. My feet don't lie.

Havlicek had an outstanding game for the Celtics, scoring 36 points and playing a strong defense against Bradley and, at times, Walt Frazier. Cowens played only 30 minutes, missing a good part of the second half because of five fouls. Tommy Heinsohn likes to joke that Havlicek is some kind of Martian because he never seems to perspire. Lennie Lewin of the New York *Post* insists that Havlicek relaxes after a game by running laps around the basketball floor for two hours. All I know is I just wish I had a tenth of his energy.

Saturday, April 27 (Off-day)

The two best teams in the NBA during the regular season were the Milwaukee Bucks and the Boston Celtics, and now, to the delight of the scriptwriters, they will be playing a best-of-seven series for the NBA Championship. The Bucks won two more games than the Celtics during the season, so they will have the so-called home-court advantage if the series happens to go seven games. I'm leaving for Milwaukee this afternoon, and I will work the first game there tomorrow with Jake.

Sunday, May 5 (Boston at Milwaukee)

That home-court advantage Milwaukee worked so hard for all season vanished today in less than two hours. The proud Celtics whipped the Bucks by 15 points—98 to 83—on their home court with a commanding exhibition of basketball. The Celtics ran their heads off, as always, and confused the Bucks with a harassing full-court press for the entire 48 minutes. Kareem Abdul-Jabbar had a routine game, scoring 35 points and collecting twenty-odd rebounds, but the second-highest scorer for the Bucks—forward Bob Dandridge—managed just 12 points. Oscar Robertson, hounded by Jo Jo White and Don Chaney, scored only two baskets and had great difficulty getting the ball up court to his teammates. With Lucius Allen still injured, the Bucks lack the kind of tall, speedy guard who can complement Robertson and help beat the Boston press.

Jake and I had no problems with the coaches, although I did give Tom Heinsohn a stern warning that was picked up over the parabolic microphone near the Boston bench. "Tom, I think I've heard enough of your voice for now," I said. "That's your warning." I didn't want to dampen Heinsohn's enthusiasm, I simply wanted to slow down his chatter and his facial grimaces. Heinsohn definitely has a chance to break Bob Boozer's record for Most Facial Distortions in one playoff schedule.

Late in the game John Havlicek lost his sneaker, and he sat down on the floor and put it on while play continued at the other end. It suddenly occurred to me that it was probably the longest rest Havlicek had enjoyed all season.

Tuesday, April 30 (Off-day)

Milwaukee evened the series at one game apiece by beating the Celtics in overtime. It was another super game, and Mendy Rudolph and Darrell Garretson maintained strong control throughout. I watched the game in my den and took an occasional sip of Double D. I also practiced my putting on the rug at halftime.

Friday, May 3 (Milwaukee at Boston)

Sadly, the O'Donnell-Powers partnership has ended, and tonight I will be working with Don Murphy. It was not my decision; the league makes the officiating assignments for each game. Jake was the perfect partner on the court, and we got along without incident off the court.

It was a great education for both of us. And I think we understand each other's position a little better.

For the most part it was an easy game to work as the Celtics stormed to a big lead and won by a comfortable margin. Once again the Celtics pressed the Bucks all over the court, and once again the Bucks coughed up the ball at an alarming rate. The Bucks committed 18 turnovers in the first half alone, an incredible number for a good team. Eighteen turnovers meant 36 points that Milwaukee definitely would not get and 36 that Boston might get. In fact, the Celtics turned those 18 turnovers into 22 points.

So strong and so successful was the Boston press that the Celtics managed to survive the long idleness of Dave Cowens, who got into foul trouble early and had to set up light housekeeping on the bench. With Cowens in foul trouble, Tom Heinsohn had to use Henry Finkel, the 7-foot center whose normal playing time amounts to a minute or two every other game. Instead of rallying while Cowens sat on the bench, though, the Bucks continued their lackluster play. In fact, Finkel even hit a couple of long shots from the top of the key when Kareem Abdul-Jabbar dared him to shoot by laying back near the basket and giving Finkel plenty of room. Each time Finkel scored with one of his long bombs, the Boston Garden crowd exploded with cheers.

If the Bucks had closed the score during Cowens' absence, Murphy and I might have had more problems than we did with respect to the one major incident that marred the game. The Celtics were leading by about 20 points at the time, and I was the trail referee, standing about twenty feet out from the foul line toward center court. Mickey Davis of the Bucks cut through the lane without the ball, hoping to sneak into an open position for a pass and an easy basket. Seeing Davis, Don Nelson of the Celtics headed after him. Nelson spotted a pick set up by one of the Milwaukee forwards, so he avoided it by going around the player. Well, Davis collected a pass, but when he put the ball to the floor and took his first step, he ran squarely into Nelson, catching the Boston player with his right shoulder. I immediately blew my whistle and called an offensive foul on Davis, at the same time waving off the basket. Then, I heard a commotion behind me and noticed that Murphy was signaling that the basket was good. Oh, no!

There was no doubt that I blew my whistle before Don blew his, and it was apparent that he hadn't heard mine. According to the rules, the foul I called on Davis negated the foul that Murphy had called on Nelson. I walked over to the scorer's table, and while I was standing there, Larry Costello, assistant coach Hubie Brown, trainer Bill Bates and several others from the Milwaukee bench surrounded me and asked what happened. So I told them: my foul preceded Murphy's foul, and that was that.

"The foul takes precedence over the violation," Costello argued.

"What violation?" I asked. "There was no violation. It was a foul. I saw something—and I called it."

Costello continued to argue and soon went beyond the boundaries of fair play.

"I want to see only one man here," I announced to the Milwaukee delegation. "The captain!" Then I told Oscar Robertson that if Costello didn't go back to his bench "it" would happen. Costello did not return to the bench and I gave him the technical, as promised.

When Costello finally stopped his harangue and went back to the bench, I thought the fight was over. But suddenly, there was Hubie Brown telling me what a stupid call I had made and how bad I was and a few things more. I must admit that Brown did not use profanity at the time, but I thought that he had gone beyond his bounds. So I gave him a technical, and ejected him from the game which under the circumstances was perfectly within the rules. John Havlicek took the two technical-foul shots—Costello's and Brown's—and missed one of them.

At halftime Wayne Embry, the general manager of the

Bucks, growled at Murphy and me as we walked off the court. Naturally I growled back. Hubie Brown had stationed himself at the dressing room door and when we arrived told me I had embarrassed him on nationwide television by ejecting him from the game. I had embarrassed him? What had he done to me? Then, for no reason, Brown began to swear—*really* swear! He cursed me within earshot of perhaps a hundred spectators. When Murphy finally shut the dressing-room door, I could still hear him screaming at me from the corridor.

Murphy was genuinely depressed about the whole scene. "Murph," I said, "you could have been right and I could have been wrong. The point is this: I called it first, so that nullifies whatever you did." Then there was a knock on the door. It was Wayne Embry, who wanted to apologize for his comments. I accepted his apologies. "Hell," Embry said, "here I'm bitching about one call when my team commits almost thirty turnovers in the game. We can't blame the referees for anything, not the way we played."

Sunday, May 5 (Off-day)

Once again the Bucks surprised the Celtics, beating them in the fourth game at the Boston Garden and tying the series at two games apiece. In the second quarter Milwaukee held Boston to only 12 points, an incredible low for a running, fast-breaking team such as the Celtics. And whatever happened to the home-court advantage? Both teams have now split at home and on the road.

Monday, May 6 (Off-day)

Maurice Podoloff was the original president of the NBA—the man who really made the NBA major league. He was recently invested into the Basketball Hall of Fame in

Springfield, Massachusetts. At the time, I wrote Mr. Podoloff a letter of congratulations. This morning Ms. Connie Maroselli, the manager of the NBA's offices in New York who has been around basketball for about twenty-five years and probably knows more about the game than most of the people in it, called me to say that she had seen Mr. Podoloff on the weekend and that he sent his best wishes.

She also said she had read my letter to Mr. Podoloff because he had been unable to decipher the Powers scribble. I had told Mr. Podoloff that everything I have now with respect to basketball, financial achievement and my status as a human being, was owed in part to him. Podoloff always treated me with the utmost respect and courtesy. I love that man.

Tuesday, May 7 (Boston at Milwaukee)

I'm sure that the people who watched the coast-to-coast telecast of the fifth game of the Boston-Milwaukee series probably thought they were watching a video-taped replay of Game One. Once again the improbable became the routine as the Celtics, resorting to their pressing defensive tactics, whipped the Bucks 96–87 on the Milwaukee court and took a commanding three-to-two lead in the championship confrontation. As always, John Havlicek and Dave Cowens dominated the game for the Celtics, while Jo Jo White and Don Chaney continued to harass the Milwaukee playmakers to the point where the Bucks began handing the ball to the Celtics on silver platters. And I don't want to forget Paul Silas and Don Nelson, the quietly effective forwards who always pick off the key rebounds and provide a clutch basket when the Celtics need it most.

Cowens seems to have adopted a sound tactical posture for his battle with Kareem Abdul-Jabbar. In fact, Cowens seems willing to concede Jabbar his 30 or 35 points and his 15 or 20 rebounds. But at the same time he is forcing

Jabbar to chase him around the court at breakneck speed and in so doing he's tiring the big man out. Statistically, Jabbar has scored more points and collected more rebounds than Cowens in this series, but I think Cowens has more than neutralized Jabbar throughout the five games played so far. In this game, for instance, Jabbar scored 37 points, but Cowens countered with 28 points. And Boston won the game, too. Right now I can't say it looks too good for the Bucks, because the sixth game will be played in the Boston Garden.

Wednesday, May 8 (Off-day)

On the flight back to New York Pat Summerall told me that Rick Barry had been highly critical of a foul I had called on Jabbar for hitting Don Chaney with his right arm. In fact, when I called the foul Barry stated over the air that there had been no foul. Then they showed an instant replay of the action between Jabbar and Chaney, and suddenly it was apology time. Barry made his "no foul" call after watching the play from about sixty feet away, while I made my call after watching it from about five feet away. Well, the replay verified the foul and, to his credit, Barry apologized for saying I had blown the play.

"The next time you see Rick," I told Pat, "tell him that the apology saves him one technical foul next year."

Only joking, of course.

Friday, May 10 (Off-day)

I never usually get jealous about anything, but I was a jealous referee tonight. Armchair referee, that is. Darrell Garretson and Mendy Rudolph made every referee in America proud with their performance up in Boston as the Bucks squared the series by edging the Celtics in double overtime. It was as good a game as I've ever seen, live or on television, and Darrell and Mendy worked it perfectly. Jabbar won the game for the Bucks when he threw in a sky hook from way out along the side in the closing seconds of the second overtime.

So now the season is down to one game: Sunday afternoon in Milwaukee. And I'll be working the game with Mendy Rudolph.

Saturday, May 11 (Off-day)

I flew to Milwaukee at dinnertime, and bumped into Darrell Garretson, the alternate referee tomorrow, in the hotel lobby. I congratulated him on his outstanding exhibition last night in Boston. Then I flaked out in my room while trying to watch an older-than-old movie about some socialite dowager with emotional problems. I think she got married in the end.

Sunday, May 12 (Boston at Milwaukee)

As one of the local papers noted his morning, Mendy and I sport contrasting records in the final series. The Celtics have won all three games that I have worked, while the Bucks have won the three games Mendy has officiated. If form holds true, the Celtics and Bucks will play three billion overtime periods this afternoon—then the Portland Trail Blazers or the Philadelphia 76ers will be declared champions of the NBA. I woke up early, naturally, and tried to do the crossword puzzles at breakfast. I managed to get through the puzzles in the Milwaukee papers without much problem, so I walked downtown at 9:30 A.M. and bought an early edition of the *New York Times*. No way I could do the *Times* puzzle, no way. I'm not as smart as I think.

I reached the arena at 12:20, some 70 minutes before the start of the game. Walter Kennedy accompanied me into the dressing room and looked around for Mendy Rudolph. No Mendy. Mendy arrives at the dressing room exactly one hour before game time. No earlier. No later.

Mendy and I didn't have much to discuss before the game. We both knew the problems confronting us in the game. We had both been here—that is, officiating seventh games—before. Frankly, as the junior member of the Rudolph-Powers firm, I always defer to Mr. Rudolph anyway.

However, Mendy does not toss the ball, because he was accidentally knocked over during a tap play years ago, so I had the privilege of beginning the game with the toss-up. "Let's not screw it up," I said to myself, and, thank heavens, I made a good toss. Jabbar tapped it backwards and right into the hands of one of the Celtics for an easy breakaway basket for Boston.

For a long time both clubs showed the pressure of a "big game." The Jabbars, the Havliceks, the Cowenses, the Robertsons, they all can feel pressure. On one play, Oscar Robertson went down on the floor in a heap, but Mendy rightfully called a block on him. Oscar leaped to his feet and charged at Mendy, but I managed to get between them. Oscar stopped, but said nothing. Still, the tenseness was evident. I patted Robertson on the hip, trying to calm him down. Then Tommy Heinsohn jumped all over me for letting Oscar go too far with his protestations. "Hey!" I said to Heinsohn, "Everyone's been going too far in this period. It'll be over soon." Sure enough, once the first quarter ended, the nervousness ended, too, and from that point on the teams played pure, crisp basketball.

With Cowens more than holding his own against Jabbar, and with Havlicek running all over the court, the Celtics pulled away to a 53 to 40 lead at halftime. However, Jabbar rallied the Bucks in the third quarter, and they closed the Celtics lead to just 5 points—71 to 66—at the start of the final quarter. Then the Boston machine poured it on one last time, steamrolling the weary Bucks with one final all-court surge. Soon a general depression began to hit the Bucks as they realized that it was almost over, that their year was coming to a close on the negative side of the ledger. And then it *was* over as the Celtics won the championship by routing the Bucks 102 to 87. Incredibly, Boston had won three games in Milwaukee, and only one in the Boston Garden. And the Celtics just happened to win all four games that I refereed in the climactic series.

The turning point of the final game, in my opinion, came in the second period when Cowens held Jabbar scoreless. Scoreless! Cowens, of course, had some help from his friends as the Celtics fronted Jabbar, backed Jabbar, double-teamed Jabbar, and even triple-teamed Jabbar at times, thus forcing the Bucks to look elsewhere for their shots.

C'est fini. Technically speaking, I am now among the ranks of the unemployed.

Monday, May 13 (Powers *vs.* Westchester)

I started my golf season today on the West Course at the Westchester Country Club. The first hole is a short par four, about 300 yards slightly downhill, and the pros all drive the green during the $250,000 Westchester Classic. I made a neat nine on the first hole this morning in the following order: duck-hooked drive, skulled second shot, topped third, shanked fourth, fluffed fifth into trap, wedged sixth over green, rolled seventh onto apron. I putted to within eight feet of the cup and finally holed it out from there.

I can only get better.

EPILOGUE

The golf clubs have been stored for the winter, and it's a new basketball season now. In fact, I'm beginning to think I should have waited another year to write this diary of a referee's life in the National Basketball Association. Kareem Abdul-Jabbar breaks his hand when he smashes it against a backboard in an exhibition game, of all things. I referee that game but have to retire early when I pull another muscle in my leg. Dave Cowens breaks his foot while chasing some guy named Fatty Taylor who plays for the Denver Nuggets, of all teams, in the American Basketball Association, of all leagues. Wilt Chamberlain officially retires a year after everyone else in basketball thinks he has retired. Cazzie Russell has knee surgery, Jeff Mullins breaks his hands. Jerry West retires, unretires, then retires again. Pistol Pete Maravich jazzes it up for an expansion team in New Orleans; Nate Thurmond rebounds for some Bulls in Chicago; and Clyde Lee returns to the south to play for Atlanta. Philadelphia wins its first two games of the season. Billy Cunningham rejoins the 76ers—and some team named the Spirits of St. Louis fine him something like $1,900 per day for jilting them. And some 19-year old kid named Drew scores 34 points for Atlanta in his first NBA game, while a vegetarian named Walton—wearing the wildest headbands and the reddest beard in the league—introduces rebounding and defense to the city of Portland.

See you under the boards. I'm the little guy with the whistle.

601

60 A   PHOTO # 40   109253

ADULT

Return this material on or before DUE DATE SHOWN BELOW to any agency of the Brooklyn Public Library system. A charge is made for each day including Sundays and Holidays, that this item is overdue. Your library card can be revoked for failure to return library material.

LAST DATE
STAMPED IS
DATE DUE

DATE DUE
OCT 1 5 1975

DO NOT
REMOVE
CARD
FROM
POCKET

THIS CARD WILL BE PROCESSED BY COMPUTER

Both cards MUST be returned in this pocket to clear your record. A charge will be made for each missing card.

60   MAY 1 2 1975

BROOKLYN PUBLIC LIBRARY
WILLIAMSBURGH
240 DIVISION AVENUE

Return this material on or before DUE DATE SHOWN ABOVE to any agency of the Brooklyn Public Library system. A charge is made for each day including Sundays and Holidays, that this item is overdue. Your library card can be revoked for failure to return library material.

BRO
DART   PRINTED IN U.S.A.